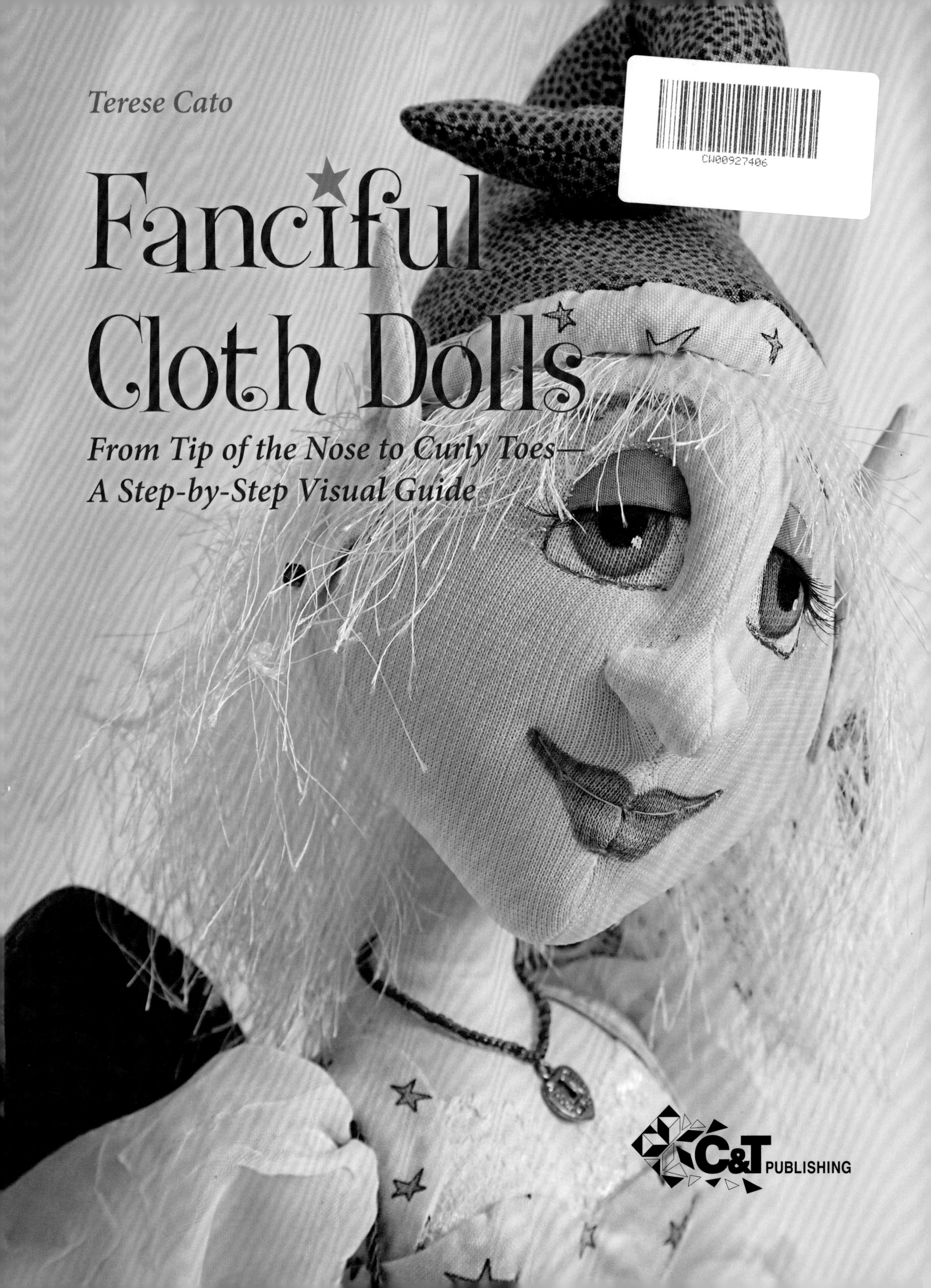
Terese Cato
Fanciful
Cloth Dolls
From Tip of the Nose to Curly Toes—
A Step-by-Step Visual Guide
CW00927406
C&T PUBLISHING

Publisher: Amy Marson

Creative Director: Gailen Runge

Art Director: Kristy Zacharias

Editors: Liz Aneloski and Phyllis Elving

Technical Editors: Ann Haley and Mary E. Flynn

Cover/Book Designer: April Mostek

Production Coordinator: Jenny Davis

Production Editor: Alice Mace Nakanishi

Illustrator: Jessica Jenkins

Photo Assistant: Cara Pardo

Photography by Diane Pedersen of C&T Publishing, Inc., unless otherwise noted

Published by C&T Publishing, Inc., P.O. Box 1456, Lafayette, CA 94549

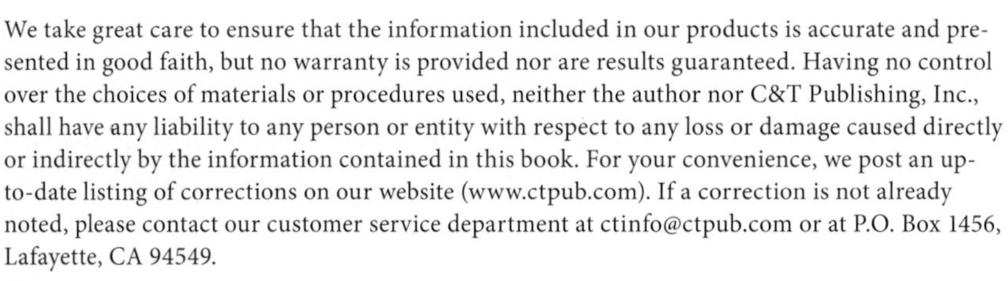

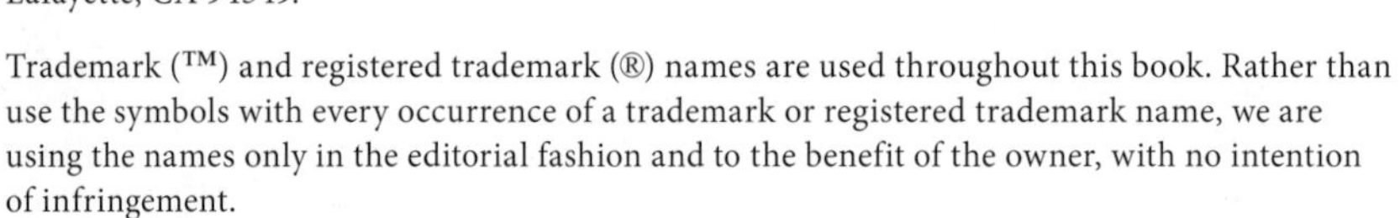

Library of Congress Cataloging-in-Publication Data

Cato, Terese.

Fanciful cloth dolls : from tip of the nose to curly toes : a step-by-step visual guide / Terese Cato.

pages cm

ISBN 978-1-60705-552-5 (soft cover)

1. Dollmaking. 2. Soft toy making--Patterns. I. Title.

TT175.C388 2013

745.592'4--dc23

2012019272

Printed in China

10 9 8 7 6 5 4 3 2

Dedication

For my mother

Contents

Preface

Do you have a treasured item that belonged to your grandmother? Perhaps your grandmother gave you something that she treasured because it belonged to *her* mother. From a tiny trinket to a beautiful quilt that adorns your bed, if the treasured item was actually made by the person it came from, then the sentimental value increases tremendously. The object may have no real monetary value, but it could be priceless to you. We consider these precious gifts to be irreplaceable.

There is a sad-looking angel that decorates my Christmas tree each year. When I say *sad,* what I really mean is *ugly.* The fact is that no matter what she looks like, she is very special to me. She has been on the Christmas tree every year since my first Christmas and I wouldn't dream of leaving her off. No one in my family made this angel. She was probably bought at a five-and-ten-cent store. But although she is not much to look at, her beauty is in her sentimental value. She holds many memories for me, so I treat her like a priceless artifact. Between Christmases, she's wrapped in tissue paper and stored in a box where no harm will come to her.

What will you pass on to or leave for your children? Will future generations of your family have something from you to hold dear to their hearts? Why not make something with the deliberate intention of creating a family heirloom? Make something worthy of becoming a prized possession to hold special memories for someone you love.

Many of our family traditions revolve around the holidays we celebrate. The customs we practice as a family remain with us our whole life. Children grow up and continue these traditions with their own families, or at least keep them as fond childhood memories. Sharing these things brings us closer together as a family.

If you're a crafter, then it's part of your nature to seek out new projects that include fun techniques. It is my intention to appeal to the crafter, sewer, and quilter in you with the projects in this book. You don't have to be a doll maker to create these projects. If you've never done anything like this before, all you need is a willingness to learn. I'll teach you the techniques and show you all the details. In this book you'll find projects that are appropriate for the beginner, the advanced crafter, and everyone in between.

I am granting you an artistic license! With this license you have complete artistic freedom to give each project special touches to make it your own. If you have skills that you enjoy—embroidery, beading, quilting—you can use them to embellish the project with a flair and style that is personally yours.

Doll-Making Basics

The most important tool for making dolls is your imagination, so pull it out and let it run wild. The second most important tool is your sewing machine. Proper routine maintenance may include cleaning, oiling, and lubricating—check the instruction booklet for your machine. Some machines are designed to be oil free, so follow the directions for your specific machine. Many problems can be avoided with routine cleaning to remove the lint, dust, and thread that can get into the working parts of a machine. If you've lost your owner's manual or bought a used machine that didn't come with one, identify the model, serial number, and age of the machine. Most manufacturers make replacement manuals available on the customer support pages of their websites.

You don't need a fancy sewing machine to create spectacular projects. If you do happen to have a fancy machine, use some of its features wherever you can. Decorative stitching on skirts, sleeves, and pants will add detail that shows you put time and thought into a project.

I get many emails asking, "Can I substitute materials?" Not only is my answer "Yes," but I *encourage* you to make substitutions. While some types of projects don't allow you to make changes to the original pattern, doll making offers many opportunities to add your personal stamp. If you feel a project pulling you in a different direction, go with it and see where you end up. You can make the same project several times and have unique results each time. The endless possibilities just add to the fun of creating.

I am also asked where I get my inspiration for projects. It's funny, but my ideas often come from what may seem like odd places. A piece of fabric, a color palette, or a prop might define the theme for me, but more often inspiration comes from a strange object that isn't even something I'll use in the project itself. I see something that triggers a memory and gets me thinking. Often these memories are from childhood. I work out all the details in my head before I begin every project. When I can see the finished project clearly in my head, I'm ready to bring my idea to life. Once in a while things get changed along the way, but only because the project is leading me in that direction. When I'm asked which doll is my favorite, my answer is always the same: It's the one I'm working on right now.

I find props around the house, down the street, and across the country. I love to travel, because it broadens my world and my opportunity to go on treasure hunts. My props can be purchased items, but most often they are *found objects*. My friends often save things they think I might use to make something. Sometimes I find an item that's perfect as is, and other times I find things that I will make into something. I put all these little treasures into a box where they wait to become part of my next project. The patterns in this book are ***not intended for young children***. All the details that make the dolls so special are not safe for children to play with.

General Sewing Equipment

Sewing machine

Open-toe or clear presser foot for sewing on traced lines

Straight pins

Sharp scissors (If you're a quilter, you may find your rotary cutter and acrylic rulers also come in handy.)

Tape measure

All-purpose sewing thread

Quilting thread for attaching body parts and sculpting doll faces

Seam ripper

Needles for hand sewing, including curved needles and 5″ and 7″ doll-making needles

Iron for pressing doll clothes

General Doll-Making Equipment

Mechanical pencil for tracing templates onto fabric

Fabric marker with disappearing ink

Reverse-action tweezers or hemostat clamp for turning body parts and making fingers (You can find these online, or look for the tweezers in the scrapbooking department of a craft store. While I prefer using the tiny turning tubes for most tasks, including turning the bigger body parts, a pair of reverse-action tweezers will come in handy for guiding a pipe cleaner into a finger. This is a matter of personal preference, so try using whatever you have on hand before buying new tools.)

Tiny turning tubes for turning fingers, body parts, and clothing (see Resources, page 95)

Stuffing tool, such as an unsharpened pencil, a chopstick, or a dowel

Wire cutter for cutting pipe cleaners for fingers

Pliers for bending pipe cleaner ends

White craft glue for assembling props

Embroidery thread for creating doll faces and gathering sleeves and pantaloons

Artist-quality watercolor pencils, available in the art section of a craft store in boxed sets or individually

Paintbrushes with stiff, blunt bristles—a larger one for wetting fabric and blending cheek color, a smaller one to blend eye and lip colors

Basic Sewing Tips

There are a few instructions that won't be repeated for each pattern but are important to note. I do the following things for all of my projects:

- Always backstitch at the beginning and end of a seam to lock the stitches and prevent them from unraveling.
- Sew with a ¼″ seam allowance unless the project directions indicate that a smaller seam allowance is required.
- Have the iron handy while you are sewing. Press open the seam allowances in clothing for a finished look. *Don't* press open the seams on body parts.
- Clip seam allowance curves so the seam can spread and lie flat once the piece is turned right side out. If the seam allowance is trimmed to ⅛″, there's no need to clip. For example, if you are working with a fabric that frays easily, use the clip method instead of trimming the seam allowance.
- Take the time to change thread while sewing. Try to match the thread color to the fabric. White thread is great, but not for everything. If you choose a dark color for the body fabric, white thread may be very noticeable after the pieces are stuffed.
- Use an appropriate stitch length. The smaller the piece you are sewing, the smaller the stitch length should be. A tight curve on a small pattern piece will be smoother if sewn with more stitches. Many of the items in this book may be smaller than pieces you normally work with, so don't forget to adjust the stitch length as needed.
- Choose the best presser foot for the job. I use the trace-sew-cut technique in many of the patterns in this book. Sewing on a traced line is easier when you use an open-toe or clear presser foot.
- Copy the template patterns onto cardstock to make them easier to trace and longer lasting.
- Use the proper tracing tool. To trace templates onto fabric, I use a mechanical pencil with fine (0.5mm) lead. This allows me to sew directly on the line. On dark fabrics, however, it can be difficult to see a traced pencil line. A tailor's white chalk pencil makes sewing traced lines on dark fabric easy.
- All the template patterns in this book are full size, so there is no need to enlarge them before copying. Check the template size to choose fabric with an appropriate scale for the project.
- To remove a pucker or ripple in the seam of a stuffed body part, rub the seam over a hot iron to smooth it out.

Making the Doll's Head

The next few pages will take you through the steps you'll follow to make a head, sculpt a face, and color a face. I'm using the Tooth Fairy (page 20) and Lyle the Elf (page 52) as examples. These dolls have different-shaped heads, but the basic construction is the same.

1 Trace the Head Front and Head Back templates (pages 78 or 89) on the wrong side of doubled fabric (2 layers of fabric placed with right sides together).

2 Note the sewing lines (dashed lines) and the cutting lines (solid lines) on the template patterns. Sew the pieces, stitching along the dashed sewing lines *only.*

3 Cut out the head front and back along the stitching, leaving a scant ¼″ seam allowance. For the areas that are not stitched, cut directly on the traced solid lines.

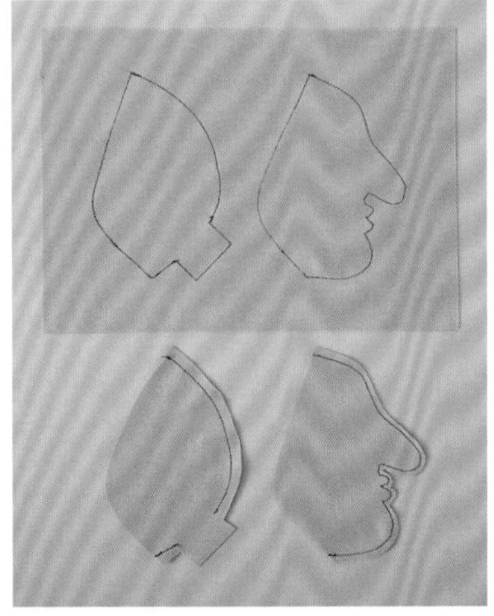
The back and front head pieces for Lyle the Elf have been sewn with red thread for clarity in the photograph.

4 With right sides together, pin the head front to the head back. Line up the front center seam with the back center seam. Use plenty of pins so the fabric won't be stretched as you sew. (See the Pincushion Girl photo on page 43.)

5 Sew around the head with a ¼″ seam allowance.

6 Turn the head right side out and stuff firmly with fiberfill. Push your finger up into the stuffed head to create a hole for inserting the neck.

Tip *Whether a doll's nose is large or small, it can be difficult to keep its stuffing firm while you stuff the head. The stuffing falls out of the nose, and after the head is stuffed it's difficult to push it back in. My solution is to stick straight pins through the nose as I stuff. The pins hold the stuffing in the nose until the rest of the head is stuffed. When the firmly stuffed head is pushing against the nose, keeping everything in place, the pins can be removed.*

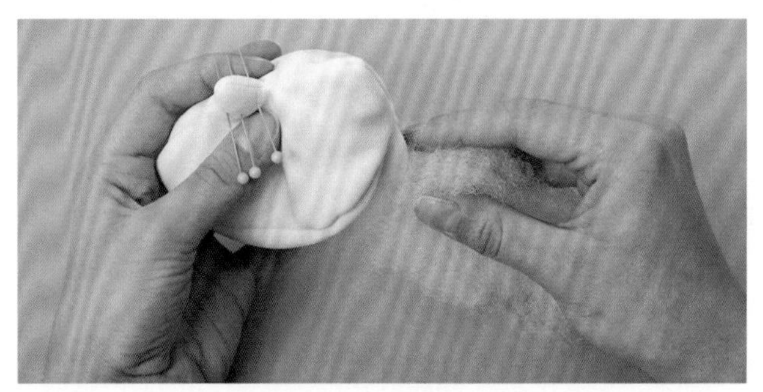
Hold the nose between your fingers as you stuff so you don't stick yourself with the pins.

Sculpting the Face

Both the Tooth Fairy and Lyle the Elf have sculpted faces. *Sculpting* may sound very artistic and difficult. For my dolls, sculpting requires only a few additional stitches, but this small effort provides additional dimensionality and personality. Take it one step at a time and you will be surprised how easy it is.

The heads are sculpted with a strong quilting thread in a color to match the fabric. Use a blue water-soluble fabric marker to draw the sculpting lines. The marks will disappear when the face is painted after sculpting.

Sculpting will define the facial features. The placement, size, and shape of the features will all come together to give the doll its own unique look. The seam in the center of the face creates right and left sides that should be as symmetrical as possible. Whatever you do on one side should be mirrored on the other side in placement, size, and shape.

All the sculpting stitches will start and stop on the seam at the back of the head behind the hairline. Knotting the thread on this seam will anchor it and hold the thread tension while you work. The tension on the thread will create a dent in the back, but the knot will be hidden later by the hair and hat. Use a 5″ or 7″ needle so you can reach the sculpting stitches easily from the back. Sew with a length of thread that's comfortable for you; start a new length as needed.

1. Use the Eye templates (pages 78 and 88) or make your own eye shape, and trace it onto the doll with a water-soluble marker. The eyes are spaced about ¾″ apart, using the seam in the face as the center line. The traced eyes may seem too far apart, but the sculpting stitches will pull them closer together. Increasing or decreasing the space between the eyes or tilting the eyes to the side will give the face a different look.

2. Draw a half-circle on each side of the nose for a nostril. Nostrils can be very round or more narrow. Extend each nostril the same distance from the center seam. You may want large nostrils on a big nose, smaller nostrils on a small nose.

3. Make a dot on the bottom of each nostril for the nostril hole. Creating an indentation for the nostril hole is optional—the doll will also look fine without it.

4. For the lips, make 2 dots on each side of the center seam, angling up slightly to form a smile.

The smaller head (*top*) belongs to the Tooth Fairy; the larger head is Lyle the Elf.

Sculpting the Lips

1. Make a knot at the back of the head (anchored to the seam) and bring the needle out on the front center seam between the lips.

2. Push the needle back in at the first dot to the *right* of the center seam and come out again at the back of the head.

3. Use your finger to push the lip in where you made the stitch while you pull the slack out of the thread. Knot the thread at the back of the head after each stitch to hold the tension.

NOTE

While sculpting, always indent the stitched area with your finger and *then* pull out the slack in the thread. If you just pull on the thread, it may break or create a hole in the fabric. If the thread *does* break, only the stitches made since the last knot are in danger of coming loose. Carefully pull out the loose stitches one at a time and begin with a new length of thread. Knotting the thread at the back of the head helps hold the tension on a stitch. It's a good idea to knot the thread before moving to a new sculpting area.

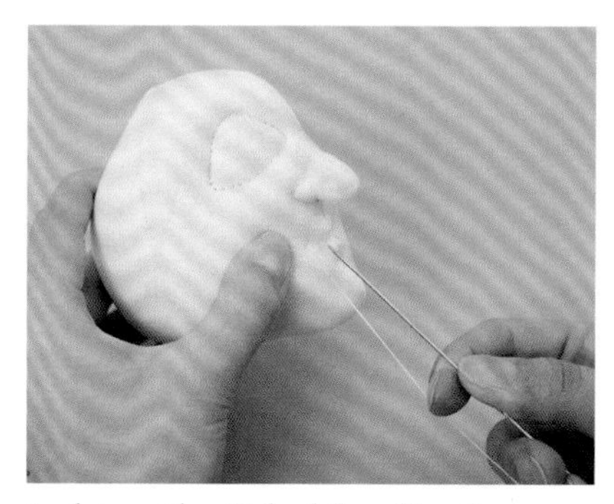

Push in on the stitch while pulling the thread taut.

If your thread is continually breaking, then you are pulling incorrectly on the stitches. Always use your finger to push in on the stitch area before you pull out the slack in the thread. If you do this correctly, there's no danger of breaking the thread.

4. Go in at the back of the head and bring the needle out at the front center seam between the lips in the same spot where you started the last stitch.

5. Go in at the first dot to the *left* of the center seam and come out at the back of the head.

6. Use your finger to push in the stitch on the lip while pulling the thread taut. Adjust the thread tension so the mouth stitches are even. Knot the thread at the back of the head.

7. Bring the needle out through the second dot on the right side and go back in at the hole made by the previous stitch. Bring the thread to the back of the head and knot it.

8. Bring the needle out through the second dot on the left side and go back in at the hole made by a previous stitch. Bring the thread to the back of the head and knot. Add a new length of thread, if needed, or continue to the next step, sculpting the nose.

Sculpting the Nose

1. The tops and bottoms of the nostrils are sculpted by stitching from the top to the bottom as follows. Go in with the needle at the back of the head and bring it out at the bottom of the right nostril, on the mark closest to the center seam of the face.

2. Make a tiny stitch (about 1/8″) and come back out at the top of the nostril, on the mark closest to the center seam (directly above the stitch you've just made).

3. Make another tiny stitch (1/8″) and bring the needle out at the stitch on the bottom of the nostril. Pinch the nostril with your fingers to pull the slack out of the thread. Make 4 tiny stitches this way and then bring the thread to the back of the head and knot.

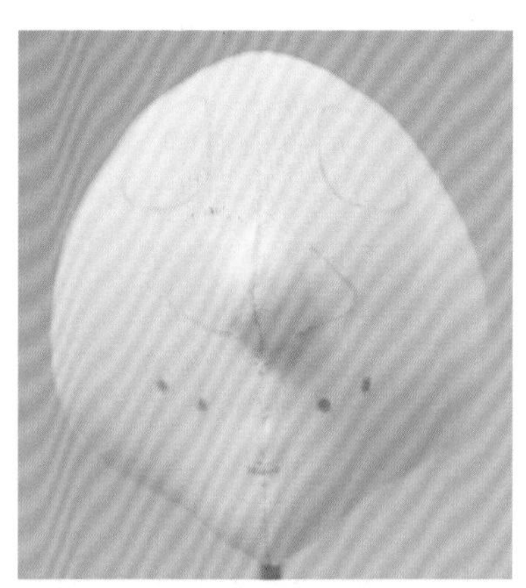

Draw nostrils before sculpting.

4. Repeat Steps 1–3 for the left nostril.

5. The outer curves of the nostrils are stitched from side to side. Go in at the back of the head and come out at the last stitch you took on the outside (top) of the right nostril.

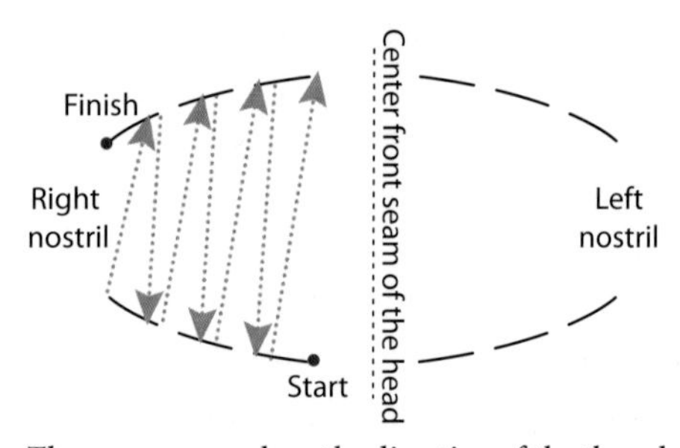

The gray arrows show the direction of the thread under the fabric. For full nostrils, insert the needle deep enough to scoop up some stuffing.

6. Make a tiny stitch and then, going through the nose from right to left, bring the needle out at the last stitch you made on the outside (top) of the left nostril.

7. Sew back and forth, making 3 stitches on each nostril. Changing the direction of the sculpting stitches will round the sides of the nostrils.

8. If you wish, you can add a stitch to create an indentation for the nostril hole. Start at the back of the head and come out where you want the nostril hole to be. Take a tiny stitch and then knot the thread at the back of the head to hold the tension. Repeat for the second nostril hole.

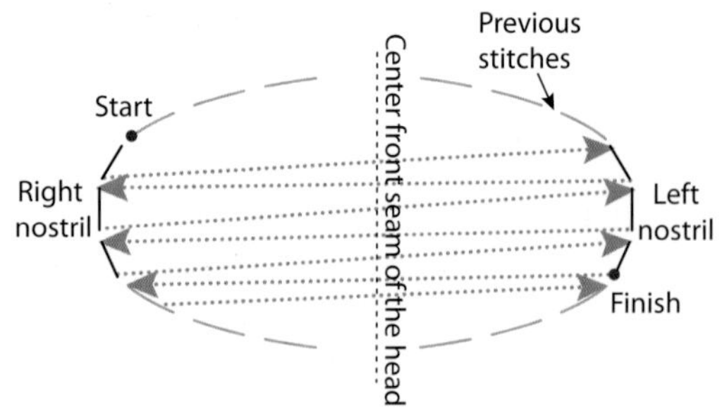

Change the stitch direction to round the sides of the nostrils.

Sculpting the Eyes

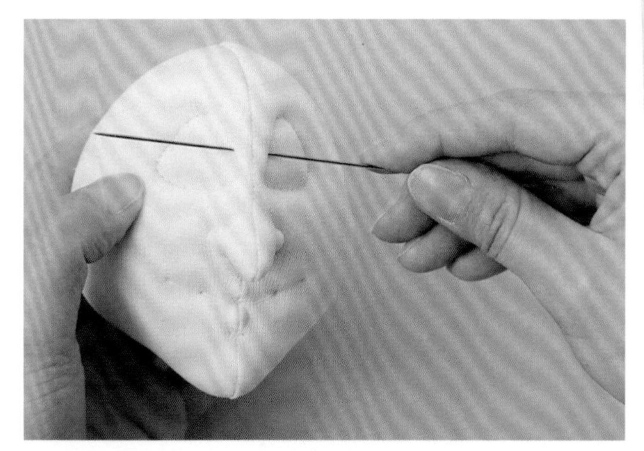

Sculpting the eyes will create the bridge of the nose.

1 Begin by knotting the thread on the seam at the back of the head. Bring the needle out on the right eye where the tear duct would be.

2 Make a tiny stitch, go in through the nose, and come out where the tear duct would be on the left eye.

3 Stitch back and forth through the nose from right eye to left eye. This will create the bridge of the nose. Keep the size of the stitches consistently small. Pinch the nose with your fingers while pulling the slack out of the thread.

4 When you get to the top of the eye, continue around the eye on the traced line, sewing back and forth from eye to eye.

5 When you have stitched around the entire eye, knot the thread at the back of the head.

Working with Watercolor Pencils

Watercolor pencils let you draw with precise control and achieve great detail. While regular colored pencils are made with a base of wax or oil, watercolor pencils have a water-soluble base that allows you to blend the colors using water. You can purchase them in a set or individually in the art department of your favorite craft store.

I enjoy teaching workshops, and I believe that I often end up learning more than my students do. When you understand something, it can be difficult to view it through the eyes of someone who is seeing it for the first time. Teaching allows me to experience firsthand how people comprehend my written words. When it comes to coloring doll faces, I always hear people say, "But I'm not an artist." The approach I take to teaching is less like an art class and more like a *process.*

Experience is the best teacher here, so don't put too much pressure on yourself to be perfect. Make a doll head just for practice. If you've never done this before, then you can't possibly know what to expect when you touch wet fabric with a watercolor pencil for the first time. Have some fun experimenting before you sit down to create your first face. You'll be amazed at the progress you can make with a little practice.

Practice with a stuffed head and two cups of water. Use one cup of water for cleaning your brushes and the other for applying clean water to the fabric.

1 Wet the fabric with a paintbrush. The fabric should be damp to the touch before you begin. After you apply the water, the fabric may be too wet, and you may need to wait a few minutes until it is *just damp.* Recognizing the difference between *wet* and *damp* is an important part of the process. If the colors bleed readily, you know the fabric is too wet. If the colors don't flow and blend easily, you know the fabric is too dry. You will also learn that some colors bleed more readily than others.

2 Color with the tip and the side of the pencil. Blend colors using a paintbrush. (It's easier to blend colors applied with the side of the pencil than colors drawn with the tip.) Add more color to the same area and blend again.

- After being blended on the fabric, some colors may look different than they look as pencil lead. Test different colors. Try blending colors together. Try blending reds, pinks, and oranges that you might use for cheek colors to see how they look on the fabric.
- Experiment by dipping the tip of the pencil in water and then coloring with it. Notice how much pigment comes off the wet pencil lead.
- Touch the pencil to the fabric using a very light hand. It is possible to erase lightly drawn lines using a paintbrush in a scrubbing motion. Light brown (terra cotta) is easily erased, so it's a great choice for drawing the outlines of eyes and lips.
- Adding a lot of shading to a face can leave a watermark when the fabric dries. Wetting the face beyond the side seams ensures that if a watermark appears, it will be under the hairline.

Note: In my experience, many white pencils do not transfer well onto fabric. If you have this difficulty, you can dip the tip of the white pencil in water before applying. Fortunately, white pencils usually don't bleed as much as many other colors.

3 Follow your project's directions for coloring eyes and lips. Practice each a few times.

4 Let your practice head dry (or speed up the process with a hair dryer). Notice how much lighter the colors look when the fabric is dry.

Coloring the Face

Both the Tooth Fairy and Lyle the Elf have eyes that are colored with watercolor pencils. The shape of the eyes is a bit different, but the process of coloring them is the same.

When you look at people's eyes, you will notice that the eyelid covers the top edge of the iris. The amount of iris that's covered depends on the shape of the eyelid and the expression on the face. Both of these dolls have fabric eyelids that are attached to the eye. For this reason, the entire iris is drawn, with the anticipation that part of it will be covered by the eyelid.

I've explained the facial features individually in the section that follows, but you will actually color the entire face (eyes, cheeks, shading, and lips) at the same time. Wet the entire face just past the side seams to prepare it for coloring and blending.

Coloring the Eyes

Color both eyes at the same time. Working on them together will help you to draw a matched set.

1 Use a large paintbrush to wet the entire face. If the fabric feels too wet, wait a few minutes until it is just damp.

2 Outline the eyes with a light brown (terra cotta) pencil, drawing with a very light touch. If you are making the Tooth Fairy or Lyle the Elf and you've sculpted the outline of the eyes, the sculpting stitching will serve as the outline.

3 Draw the iris as a complete circle that reaches the outline of the eye at the top and bottom. If the shape of the eye is tall, then the shape of the iris may be more of an oval than a circle.

4. Color in the whites of the eyes.

5. Decide what color the eyes will be and choose light, medium, and dark pencils in that color. Also choose a yellow to highlight the iris. Outline the iris in the dark pencil. Color the top half of the iris dark, one-quarter of it medium, and the final quarter with the light pencil and the yellow pencil, as shown.

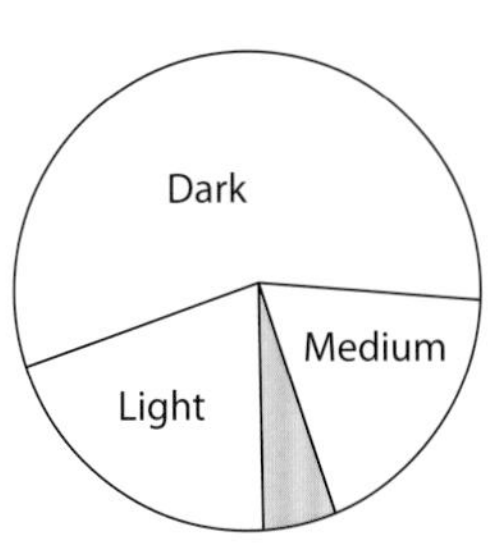

Use three shades, plus yellow, to color the iris.

6. With a small paintbrush, blend the colors of the iris. You can add more color, but be sure to add the same color to both eyes. You might also choose to divide the color sections differently than I did, and that's fine. The important thing to remember is to color both eyes just alike, working on them at the same time so they will match.

7. With a black pencil, draw a circle for the pupil and then fill it in.

8. Outline the eyes in dark brown. I typically choose dark brown over black because black can look a bit harsh—especially if you are working with a light or pale fabric for the face. You can add a touch of red to the tear duct area.

9. Finish the eyes with a dot of white. Dip a toothpick in white acrylic paint and touch it to the lower edge of the pupil to make the dot.

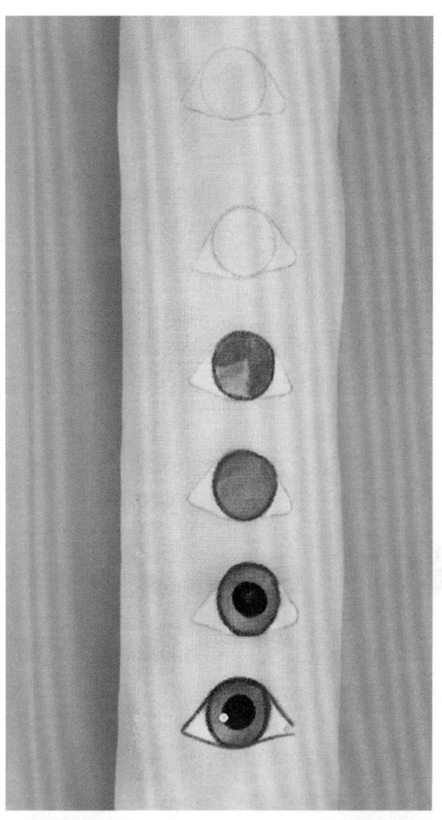

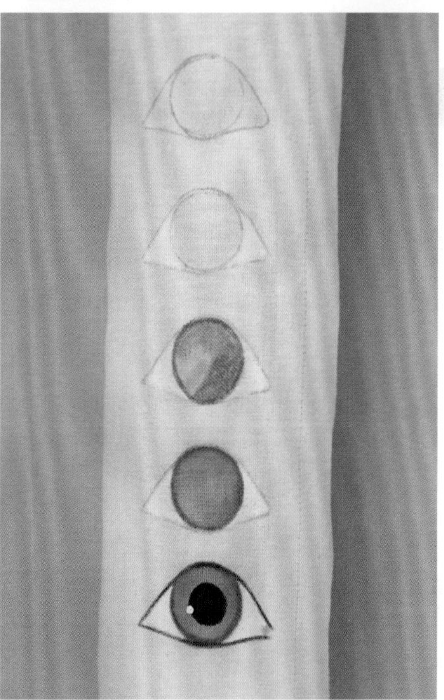

Practice coloring the eyes, step by step.

Shading the Face

You can shade the face a lot or simply add cheek color. Light shades of brown blended to the sides of the nose, cheekbones, chin, and forehead will add depth to the sculpted face. Shading can even add contour to areas that aren't sculpted.

1. Apply shading to a damp face. Use the *side* of the pencil, not the point. Blend the color using a paintbrush. If an area seems too dark or the edge is too defined, use a stiff paintbrush in a scrubbing motion to blend the color.

2. Choose a pink, red, orange, or peach pencil to add color to the cheeks. Once the color is blended into the fabric, it can appear very different than the color of the pencil lead. Blend the colors on your practice head first to test them.

3. The color will dry lighter than it looks while the fabric is damp. Apply more color on top of a previously shaded area if it needs to be darker.

Coloring the Lips

1. Use a light pink or light brown (terra cotta) pencil to draw the outline of the lips. The sculpting stitches are the separation between the top and bottom lip, and the center seam of the face divides the lips in half vertically. Draw 2 circles for the top lip and a single circle (or oval) for the bottom lip. The lips can be full or thin. The corner of the mouth can be at the sculpting stitch, or it can extend beyond. If you chose not to sculpt the mouth, draw a line for the separation between the lips. Draw lines from the circles to the corners of the mouth.

2. Use a darker lip color to outline the lips, a lighter shade to color them in.

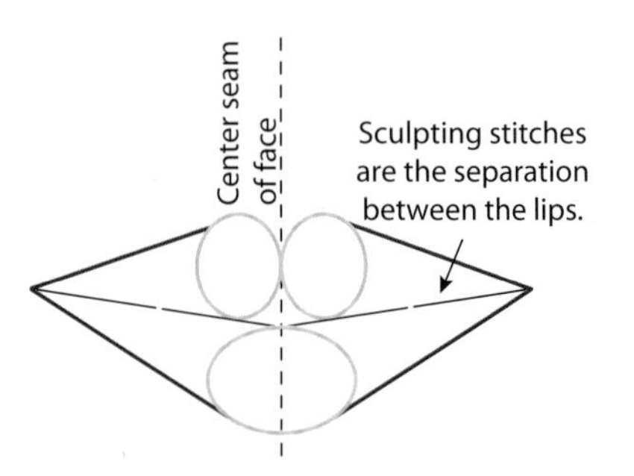

Starting with three circles makes drawing lips quick and easy.

Outline the lips and then fill them in with a lighter pencil, as shown here on the Tooth Fairy.

Coloring the Eyebrows

Since you will be coloring all the facial features at the same time, the head will still be damp as you add the eyebrows. As you choose the eyebrow color, consider the color of the hair your doll will have. Make the eyebrows very dark for dark hair or light brown for blonde hair. Use either 1 or 2 colors. With a sharp pencil, make short, quick stokes for each eyebrow.

As another option, you can stitch the eyebrows as explained for the Pincushion Girls (page 45) or use needle-felted wool as explained for Lyle the Elf (page 59).

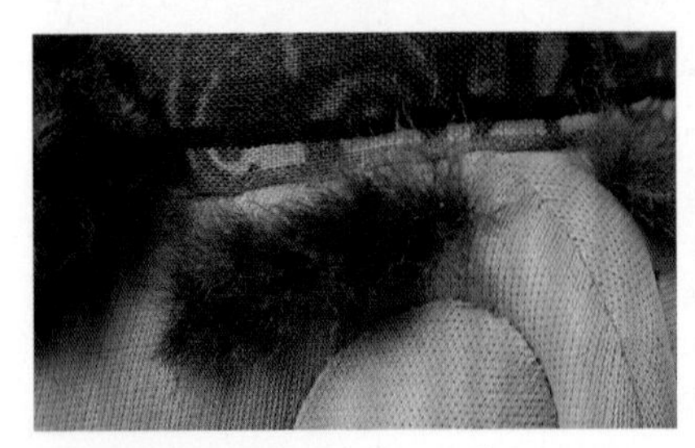

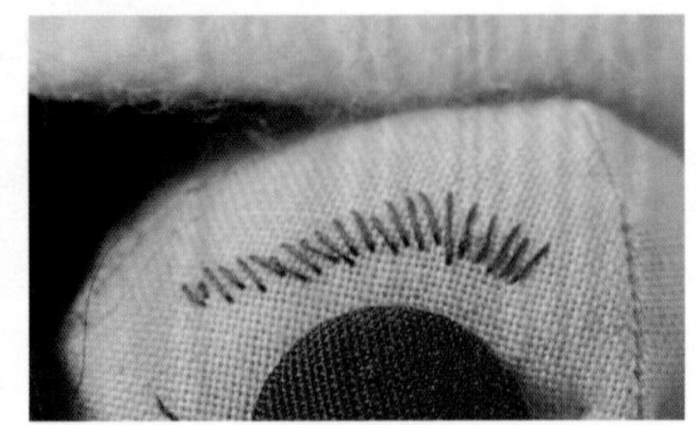

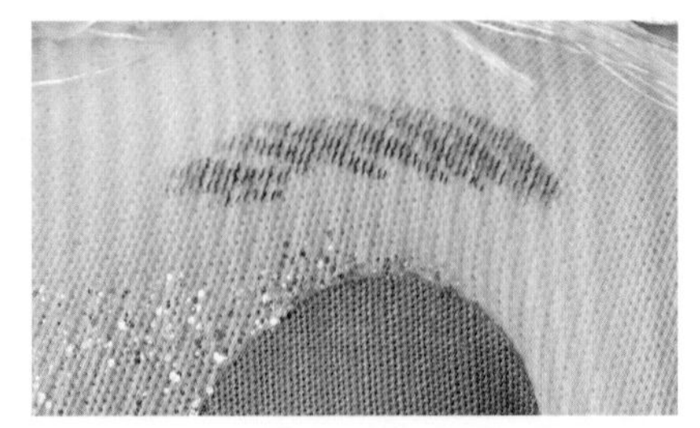

You can choose any of these eyebrow options: needle-felted wool (*left*), stitching with a single strand of thread (*center*), or drawing with watercolor pencils (*right*).

Adding Eyelids and Lashes

1. The Tooth Fairy and Lyle the Elf both have eyelids that are glued in place on top of the eye. After the doll's face is sculpted and colored, make a paper template for the eyelid—the shape of the eye but just slightly larger—to cover the upper part of the eye. Lay your eyelid template over the eye and make adjustments until the shape is right.

2. The eyelid can be the same fabric as the head or another color. Cut a 4″ × 4″ square of fabric and a 2″ × 4″ rectangle of fusible web.

3. Fold the fabric in half, wrong sides together, and press. Place the fusible web inside the folded fabric and press to fuse.

4. Use a pencil to trace the eyelid template onto the fused fabric, positioning the template so the eyelash edge is on the fold of the fabric. Cut out the eyelids.

5. Adding eyelashes is optional. Notice that Lyle the Elf (page 52) does not have eyelashes. On dolls with eyelashes, I prefer using the false eyelash bunches that you can buy at the drug or grocery store; they come in short, medium, and long sizes. Pick up an eyelash bunch with tweezers, dip the end in white craft glue, and affix to the back side of the eyelid edge. Repeat with additional bunches, gluing the same number of bunches to each lid. Let the glue dry completely before attaching the lids to the eyes.

6. Since the lid has been cut slightly wider than the eye, it will cup over the eye just a bit. Use a toothpick to apply glue to the back of the lid's upper edge (not the edge with the lashes). Position the lid carefully—the small amount of glue will adhere quickly.

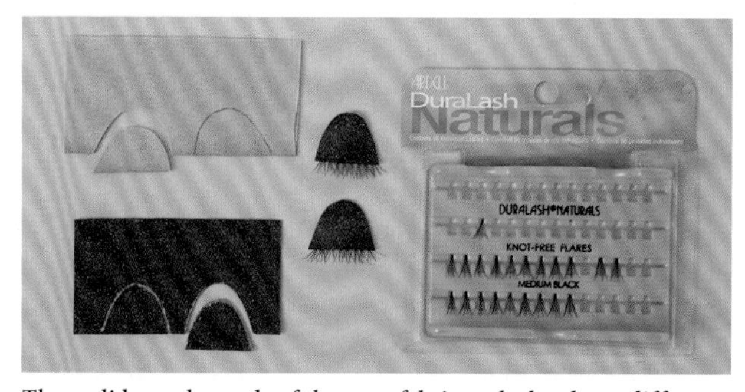

The eyelids can be made of the same fabric as the head or a different color. Eyelashes that come in small bunches let you add as many as you like.

Creating the Arms and Hands

The Tooth Fairy and Lyle the Elf have arms and hands that are made separately. They could easily have been made as single pieces, but I chose to separate the hand from the arm so the wrist can be rotated. This permits many hand positions, accommodating any object you want to place in the hand. It also allows you to create expression through the hands—as I did on my Princess Nola doll (page 36).

Making the Arms

1. On the wrong side of doubled fabric, trace 2 arms. If you are using a striped fabric for Lyle the Elf, note the direction of the stripe on the template.

2. Sew along the traced line, leaving an opening at the wrist end for turning and stuffing. Cut out the arms, leaving a ¼″ seam allowance.

3. Turn each arm right side out. Stuff firmly and turn under the raw edge of the wrist ¼″.

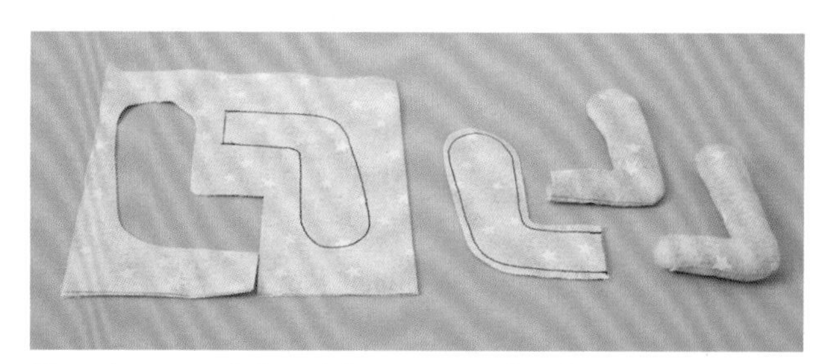

Trace the arms, stitch, and then cut out and stuff.

Forming the Hands and Fingers

1. On the wrong side of doubled fabric, trace 2 hands.

2. Sew along the traced line, using a very short stitch length. (If you can take 2 stitches between fingers, your stitch is short enough.) It's helpful to use a clear or open-toe presser foot so that you can see the traced line as you sew.

3. Cut out the hands, leaving a ⅛″ seam allowance. Cut straight down between 2 fingers, being careful not to cut into the stitches.

4. Turn the hands right side out. Tiny turning tubes will quickly and neatly turn the fingers. Turn each finger into the palm of the hand and then reach in with tweezers or a hemostat, grab a finger, and pull out gently to turn the hand right side out.

5. To wire the fingers, cut 10 pieces of white pipe cleaner. The length you need is different for each doll (1¼″ for the Tooth Fairy, 1½″ for Lyle the Elf). Use pliers to fold over the wire at both ends of each piece.

6. Insert a tiny amount of stuffing into the tip of each finger. (The solid rod from the set of turning tubes is the perfect size to use as a stuffing tool for the fingers.)

7. Use tweezers or a hemostat to guide a pipe cleaner piece into a finger, pushing it all the way to the fingertip.

8. Use tweezers to guide a small bit of stuffing into the finger. Use the solid rod of the turning tubes set to push the stuffing in. Alternate stuffing on both sides of the finger so that the pipe cleaner is surrounded by stuffing, creating a nicely rounded finger. Stuff all the fingers this way.

9. Stuff the palm of the hand firmly. Turn under the raw edge of the wrist ¼″ and finger press.

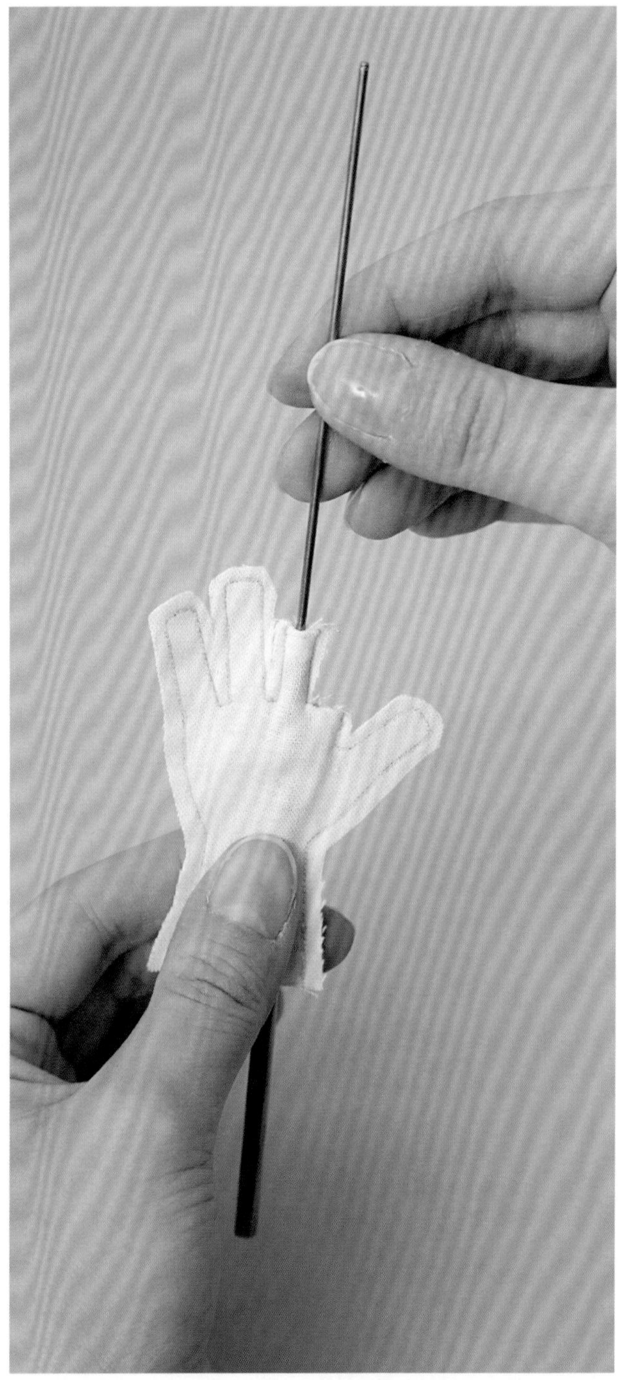

When using turning tubes, choose the largest open rod that fits into the finger.

Joining the Arms and Hands

1. Think about what you will be putting into the hands of the doll. Position the hands accordingly. Ladder stitch the hands to the arms at the wrist. Before completely closing the opening, add extra stuffing to make sure the wrist is firm.

2. Sew trim around the wrist to hide the seam where the arm meets the hand.

For the Tooth Fairy: Cut a 2½″ length of 1″-wide lace trim for each arm. The lace will become the cuff for the sleeves later. Pin the lace to the wrist with the decorative edge at the top of the hand and the straight edge on the arm. Overlap the ends of the lace on the inside of the wrist. Sew the lace to each wrist using matching thread and tiny stitches that will be hidden in the lace.

For Lyle the Elf: Use the Glove Band template to cut 2 bands. With right sides together, fold the bands in half lengthwise. Sew down the length of each band with a ¼″ seam allowance. Leave both ends open, forming a tube. Turn right side out and stuff very softly. Wrap the bands around the wrists to cover the seam between the arm and the glove, positioning them to join on the underside of the hand. Tuck in the raw edge at each end so the band meets without overlapping. Ladder stitch the band ends together. Before cutting the thread, make a few stitches through the band into the arm to hold the band in place. Add 1 or 2 buttons to each band.

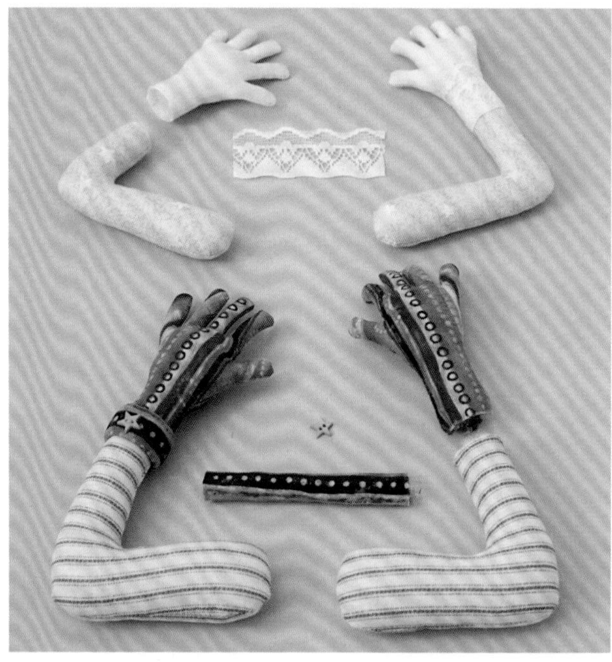

The Tooth Fairy's long sleeves (top) are edged in lace to cover the seam where the arm joins the hand. On Lyle the Elf (bottom), a band around the wrist hides the seam.

Making Doll Stands

Even if they can stand on their own, standing dolls should be secured on stands. I prefer stands in neutral colors that don't call attention to themselves. Unfinished wood plaques, readily available in different sizes and shapes, make excellent bases for doll stands.

Cut a ¼″-diameter dowel to a length that reaches to the upper back of the doll. Drill a hole in the base and glue the dowel in place in the hole, using white craft glue. Then glue a short piece of wood crosswise to the top of the dowel as a support. This can be made from a smaller dowel, a wooden barbecue skewer, a craft stick, or a coffee stirrer.

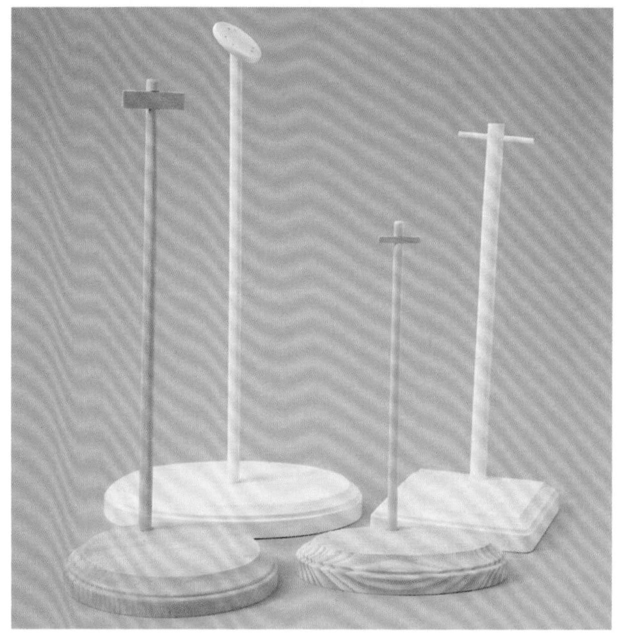

Doll stands can be painted or left their natural wood color.

The Tooth Fairy

19″ doll

While researching the story of the Tooth Fairy, I found that countries around the world have their own traditions surrounding the loss of baby teeth. In Italy the Tooth Fairy is a small mouse. In some European countries, it's traditional to bury the teeth. There are as many variations as there are countries. In the early twentieth century, the Tooth Fairy became a part of American folklore.

I asked people young and old to tell me what they knew about the Tooth Fairy. I was fascinated by the stories I heard. But when I asked what the Tooth Fairy looked like, people stopped to think. All agreed that as a *fairy* she had wings and pointed ears, but beyond that the details got a little sketchy. Children told me that she always comes when you are sleeping, so no one gets a look at her. Everyone calls her the Tooth Fairy—not one person I asked knew her real name. I found it funny that for a character that's so well known, the details of her appearance are so undefined. The upside is that you can use your artistic license and define the Tooth Fairy as you see her in your own mind.

A wonderful family tradition would be to bring out the Tooth Fairy doll when there's a loose tooth. Her body is in a flying position, so she can hang from the ceiling. She is meant to be a keepsake, not a toy, so hanging her up keeps her safe from young hands and adds to the mystery.

I've given the Tooth Fairy a tooth-shaped pouch for storing the teeth she collects. (All the children in the family need their own tooth pouches, with their names on them.) She also carries a money purse to tuck under the child's pillow. It would be appropriate for her to leave a new toothbrush, too. The next day, while no one is looking, the Tooth Fairy can be put in her box and stored away to wait for another loose tooth. Take good care of her, and this family tradition can be preserved for the next generation of children with loose teeth.

NOTE

Fabric Selection

The arms, legs, dress bodice, and hat brim are all made from the same fabric. If you choose a multicolored print, you'll have many options for bringing other fabric colors into the rest of her clothes.

Try to match the colors of the head and body fabrics. Don't be concerned if it's not an exact match—after coloring and shading the face, you won't notice the difference. Choose the polyester knit for the head first, and then match that to a cotton fabric (such as Kona Cotton) for the body. The cotton fabric will offer a wider selection of colors for matching the polyester knit.

Materials

See page 8 for lists of general sewing and doll-making equipment.

- 6″ × 16″ flesh-tone polyester knit fabric for head
- ⅓ yard flesh-tone cotton fabric for body, hands, and ears
- ¼ yard multicolor print fabric for arms, legs, dress bodice, and hat brim
- ¼ yard cotton print fabric for pantaloons
- 8″ × 16″ cotton print fabric for hat and shoes
- 5″ × 8″ scrap of cotton print fabric for shoe lining
- ¼ yard organza fabric for sleeves
- ⅓ yard cotton print fabric for wings
- 16″ of ¼″- to ½″-wide trim for pantaloons
- 8″ of 1″-wide lace trim for sleeve cuffs
- 6″ of 1½″- to 2″-wide lace trim for bra
- 4″ × 4″ scrap of fabric for eyelids
- 2″ × 4″ scrap of fusible web for eyelids
- 4″ × 8″ white print for tooth pouch (A white-on-white cotton print was used for the sample doll; use a solid white fabric if you will be applying a photo to the pouch.)
- 4″ × 8″ fabric for tooth pouch lining
- 14″ of string or ⅛″-wide ribbon for tooth pouch strap
- 4″ × 7″ cotton print fabric for money purse
- 4″ × 7″ solid-color cotton fabric for purse lining
- 9″ of string or ⅛″-wide ribbon for money purse strap
- 8″ × 25″ fine bridal netting for slip
- ¼ yard each of several colors of organza* for skirt (The sample doll's skirt was made with 5 colors of organza.)
- ¼ skein eyelash yarn for hair
- 6 white pipe cleaners for fingers, wings, and hat
- Polyester fiberfill
- Coordinating thread for sewing
- Clear thread for attaching hat
- Strong quilting thread for sculpting face (matching face color)
- Artist-quality watercolor pencils for coloring face
- False eyelash bunches (the type found in the cosmetics section of the drugstore)
- Beads for earrings, rings, and detailing on the sleeve cuffs (*optional*)
- New children's toothbrush
- 1 jump ring to sew to back for hanging (available where jewelry-making supplies are sold)

* *Organza comes in many colors—use as many or as few as you like for the Tooth Fairy's skirt. Variegated organza gives you 2 or 3 colors in a single fabric. You'll also find organza with glitter, sequins, and rhinestones attached, or you can add your own sequins and rhinestones with dots of white glue.*

Templates Required

You'll use the following templates (pages 78–83) for the Tooth Fairy:

Head Front, Head Back, Ear, Eye, Body Front, Body Front Bust, Body Back, Arm, Hand, Leg A, Leg B, Pantaloons, Bodice, Bodice Straps, Shoe, Shoe Lining, Wing A, Wing B, Hat, Tooth Pouch, Money Purse

(To make the standing Princess Nola or Housework Fairy doll pictured on pages 36 and 37, use the Leg C template.)

All templates are traced onto 2 layers of fabric placed right sides together, unless otherwise indicated.

Constructing the Body

This pattern uses the trace-sew-cut technique. The templates show both cutting and sewing lines. An arrow indicates the direction of stretch in the fabric. Find the direction of stretch in your fabric and lay out the templates accordingly.

Sewing and Stuffing the Body

1. On the wrong side of a single layer of fabric, trace the Body Front, Body Front Bust, and Body Back templates. Cut out the darts when making the templates so you can trace the dart shapes onto the fabric.

2. Sew the body front to the bust front, using a scant ¼″ seam allowance.

3. Sew the darts on the body front and back.

4. Pin the front to the back, right sides together, and sew with a ¼″ seam allowance. Leave the neck open for turning and stuffing.

5. Turn the body right side out.

6. Through the neck, stuff the body firmly with polyester fiberfill. Use a stuffing tool or dowel to pack in the stuffing, making sure to push ample stuffing into each breast. Stuff the neck firmly so it will support the head.

7. Whipstitch the neck closed. This seam will be hidden when the head is attached.

Making the Legs

1. On the wrong side of doubled fabric, trace a Leg A and a Leg B template.

2. Match thread and fabric color as closely as possible. Stitch each leg on the stitching line. Notice that there is an opening at the top of the thigh for turning and stuffing.

3. Stuff each leg firmly to just above the knee, and then stuff the top of the thigh softly so you can manipulate it to wrap around the hip. Ladder stitch the leg openings to close them.

Forming the Arms and Fingers

Follow the instructions in Creating Arms and Hands (pages 17–19).

Attaching the Bra

It takes about 3″ of lace to cover each breast. Only the top ¾″ of the lace will show once you've put on the bodice. This is a great place to use lace scraps you may have on hand.

1. Cut a 3″ length of 1½″- to 2″-wide lace trim for each breast.

2. Pin a piece of lace over each breast from the shoulder to the upper waist. Fold a dart under the breast so the lace will lie flat against the body.

3. Using thread that matches the lace so your stitches won't show, hand stitch the lace to the body. You may find a curved needle helpful.

Making the Sleeves

Your organza sleeve fabric should be soft and flowing so that it will drape nicely on the arm.

1. From the sleeve fabric, cut 2 pieces 6″ × 6½″. Fold each piece in half, right sides together, matching up the 6½″ edges.

2. Sew a ¼″ seam down the 6½″ length of each sleeve.

3. Sew a gathering stitch at each end of the sleeve, about ¼″ from the edge.

4. Slide the sleeve onto the arm. Pull the gathering threads at the wrist. Position the sleeve so that the seam is on the inside of the arm. Tuck the raw edge under at the wrist and evenly space the gathers. The edge of the sleeve will cover the edge of the lace.

5. Sew the sleeve to the lace around the wrist. Leave the top of the sleeve loose for now.

Embellishing the Cuffs

Adding beads to the cuffs—an optional detail—is easiest before the arms are attached to the body. Each bead is hand sewn to the cuff. You can make up a design or follow the design in the lace. On the sample doll, seed beads strung like a bracelet are held to the arm with tiny stitches where the sleeve meets the cuff. More beads sewn to the cuff add detail.

If you choose not to add beads, you could tie ribbon or cord around the wrist. Just remember that the time you spend adding details will help make the finished doll special.

Attaching the Arms and Legs

1. Pin the legs to the body, wrapping the softly stuffed thigh around the hip. Position the legs as if the Tooth Fairy were flying.

2. Ladder stitch each leg securely to the body.

3. Push the top of each sleeve down around the elbow, exposing the top of the arm. Pin the arms to the body at the shoulder and then ladder stitch securely in place.

4. Pull the sleeve back up around the top of the arm, making sure the sleeve seam is on the inside of the arm. Pull the threads of the gathering stitch at the top of the sleeve. Arrange the gathers evenly. Gather the sleeve so the gathering thread sits in the groove between the arm and the body. Tuck the raw edge of the sleeve under and tie off the thread.

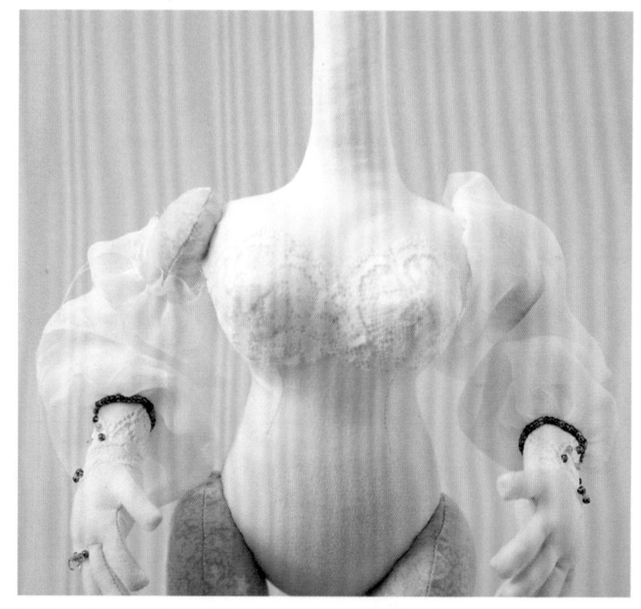

Pull up the top edge of the sleeve so it is hidden between the arm and the body.

Dressing the Doll

Pantaloons

1. Trace the Pantaloons template on the wrong side of doubled fabric.

2. Sew the crotch seam. Cut around the stitching, leaving a ¼″ seam allowance.

3. Cut 2 pieces of pantaloon trim 6″ long. Open the leg and sew trim to the right side of the fabric about ½″ from the bottom edge on each leg.

4. Fold under the raw edge of the pantaloon ½″ to reveal the trim; press.

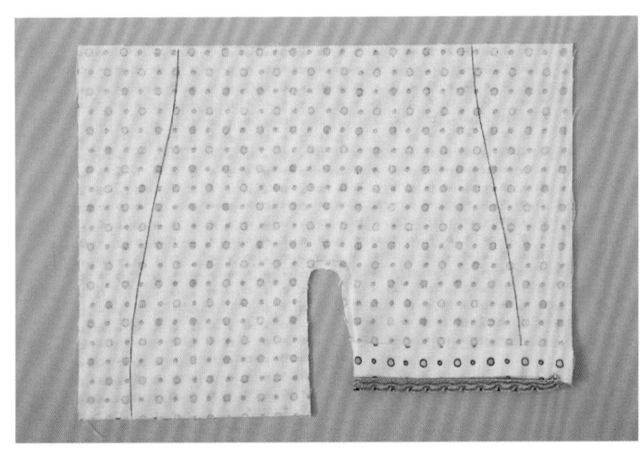

Fold under the edge of the pantaloon to show the trim.

5. With right sides together, line up the bottom edge of each pantaloon leg and pin the side seam. Sew on the traced line of both side seams.

6. Trim the side seams, leaving a ¼″ seam allowance. Cut the waist on the traced line. Cut a 1½″ opening at the center back, as indicated on the template.

7. Turn the pantaloons right side out. Fold under the raw edges of the back opening ¼″ and press.

8. Try the pantaloons on the doll. Pin the opening at the center back of the body. Line up the side seams of the pantaloons with the side seams of the body and anchor in place by sticking a pin through the pantaloons into the body. Pinch the waist of the pantaloons to form 2 darts at the back and 2 darts at the front so the pantaloons fit snugly around the waist. Mark the size and placement of each dart, using a disappearing fabric marker. Each dart is 1″ long as shown on the template.

9. Remove the pantaloons from the doll and sew the darts.

10. Put the pantaloons back on the doll. Ladder stitch the back opening closed. The skirt and bodice will hide the raw edge of the pantaloons at the waist.

11. Cut 2 pieces of ¼″ ribbon 7″ long. Tie a piece around each pantaloon leg about ¾″ up from the bottom edge.

Slip

Adding the slip will give the skirt fullness and allow the bottom edge of the pantaloons to be seen. The finer the netting you use for the slip (the smaller the holes), the softer it will be.

1. Fold the 8″ × 25″ piece of slip netting in half so that the rectangle now measures 4″ × 25″. Press the fold with a cool iron (so the netting doesn't melt).

2. Sew a gathering stitch ¼″ from the folded edge.

3. Gather the netting and pin it around the waist so that the folded edge is at the top edge of the pantaloons.

4. Arrange the gathers evenly around the waist. Slightly overlap the ends of the netting at the center back. Sew the netting to the waist, catching the body fabric in the stitches. A curved needle may be helpful for this.

The slip will make the skirt appear full and give it a nice shape.

Skirt

1 Cut strips of organza in lengths of 8″, 6″, and 4″ and in widths varying from ½″ to 1½″. Don't worry about being precise—you want the strips to be different. The number of strips is up to you. They'll be added to the skirt in 3 layers, beginning with the 8″ strips, then the 6″, and finally the 4″. The sample doll's skirt has 12 strips of each size.

2 Working near the kitchen sink and avoiding drafts that could blow out the flame, light a candle or tea light. Move the edge of a fabric piece *above the flame,* allowing the heat to melt the edge of the organza. Do not touch the melted fabric for a few moments; allow it to cool and harden. If the fabric turns black, you are holding it too close to the flame.

Hold the fabric *above the flame* and keep it moving to melt all the edges. If you hold it in one position too long, the fabric strip will melt all the way through. Keep your fingers away from the flame and the melting edge of the fabric.

Do not put the organza in the flame of the candle. Let the heat rising from the candle melt the fabric.

NOTE

It's safest to work next to the kitchen sink—if the fabric catches on fire, you can drop it into the sink. Each organza fabric may react differently to the candle's flame. Some will melt more quickly than others. Do *not* put the fabric directly into the flame.

3 Repeat the process for the remaining strips until all the edges have been melted.

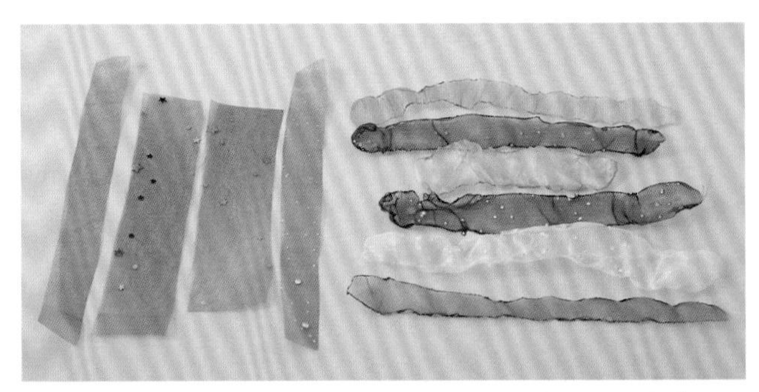

The strips at left have been cut in different sizes. Those at right have had their edges melted.

4 Pin the 8″ strips in place around the waist. The top edge of each strip should be even with the top edge of the pantaloons and the slip. Distribute the strips evenly around the waist. As you position one layer on top of another, stagger the strips (like roof shingles).

5 Stitch around the waist to attach the top edge of the strips to the body. It's best to stitch a single layer at a time. You may find a curved needle helpful for doing this.

6. Pin the 6″ strips to the waist and stitch them to the body.

7. Pin the 4″ strips to the waist and stitch them to the body.

8. If you wish, embellish the skirt further by adding sequins, rhinestones, glitter, charms, beads, or anything else you can think of. Use a toothpick to pick up a dab of white craft glue and then touch the toothpick to the skirt where you want to add something. You can also attach beads with thread.

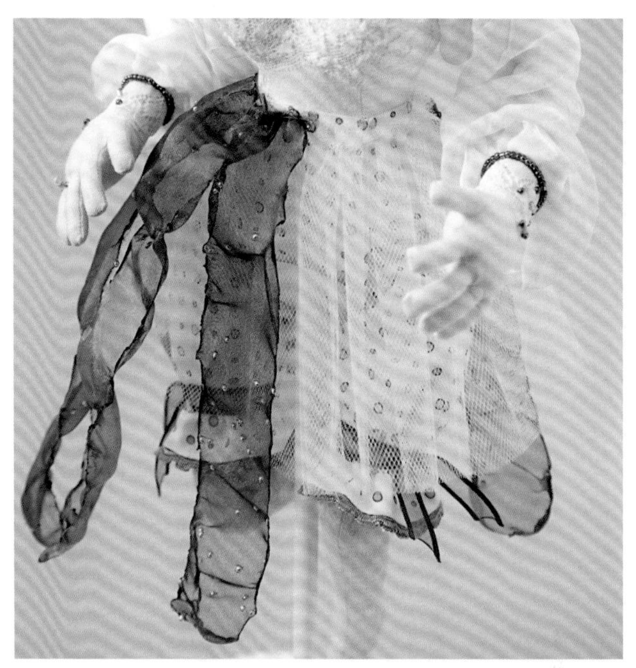

Attach the longest strips first.

Bodice

1. On the wrong side of a single thickness of fabric, trace the Bodice template.

2. Cut out the bodice ½″ outside of the traced line.

3. Sew the darts as indicated on the template.

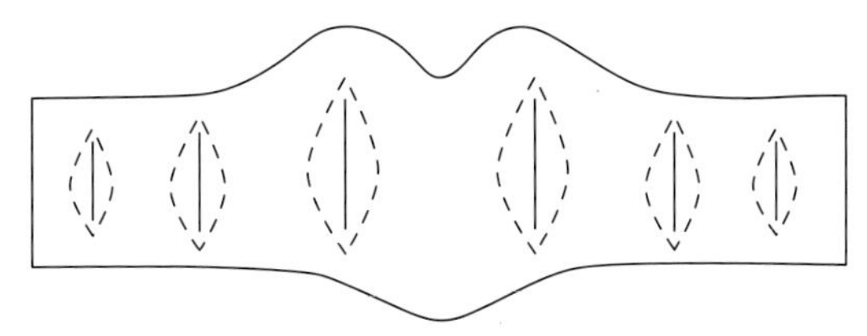

Darts allow the bodice to follow the line of the body.

4. With right sides together, pin the bodice to a second piece of fabric. Sew together on the original traced line across the top and bottom, leaving the ends open.

5. Trim the seam allowance to ¼″ and turn right side out. Press.

Bodice Straps

The bodice straps are little horseshoe-shaped pieces placed around the top of the arm, adding a Renaissance flair to the doll's costume.

1. Trace the Bodice Strap template twice on the wrong side of doubled fabric.

2. Sew both long sides of each strap on the traced line. Leave each end open, as indicated on the template.

3. Turn the straps right side out and press. Tiny turning tubes are very helpful for turning these small straps.

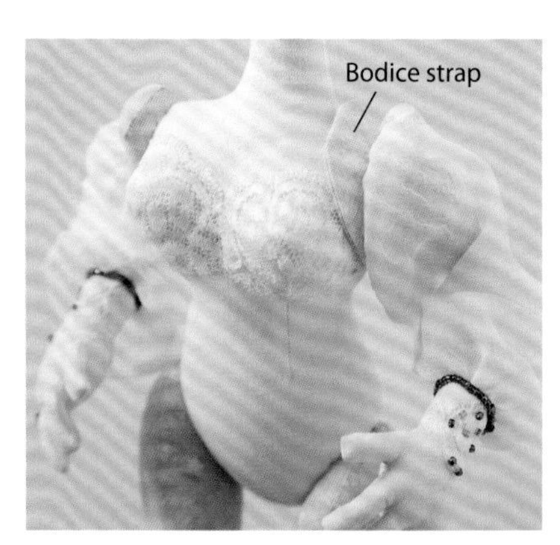

Place the bodice strap above the sleeve.

Attaching the Bodice

1 Place the bodice straps over the doll's shoulders, with the ends overlapping under the arms. Stitch the overlapping strap ends to the body to hold them in position.

2 Wrap the bodice around the body and pin in place so the bottom covers the top edge of the pantaloons and skirt pieces. Turn under the raw edges of the bodice ends so they meet in the center of the back without overlapping.

3 Ladder stitch the bodice back.

4 Sew tiny stitches along the bodice edges (around the waist and the top of each breast) to hold it in place.

Making the Shoes

1 Trace the Shoe and Shoe Lining templates on the wrong side of doubled fabric. Trace each template twice.

2 Sew around each shoe on the traced line, leaving the top edge open.

3 Cut out the shoes along the stitched line only, leaving a ⅛″ seam allowance. Do not trim the top edge of the shoes yet. Turn the shoes right side out and set aside.

4 Sew the sides of each shoe lining on the traced lines, leaving the top and bottom edges open.

5 Cut out the shoe lining, leaving a ⅛″ seam allowance along the stitched sides only. Cut the bottom of the lining on the solid line. Do not cut out the top of the lining yet.

6 Slide the lining over the shoe, right sides together. Sew together around the top edge of each shoe on the traced line. Trim the seam allowances to ⅛″.

7 Turn the lining to the inside of the shoe, allowing a little of the lining to show, and press.

Slip the lining over the shoe, stitch around the top, and turn to the inside.

8 Put a small amount of stuffing in the pointed tip of each shoe to fill out the space where the toes won't reach. Place the shoes on the doll's feet.

Choosing a contrasting color for the shoe linings really makes them pop!

Making the Wings

When it comes to making wings, you have many options. Considering that this doll will need to withstand the test of time and be stored in a box, I chose cotton fabric for my wings. Select a print that will work in harmony with your other fabric choices.

Although the wings are simple in design, they express the illusion of flight. Pipe cleaners inserted into the wings allow them to hold their position and be reshaped easily should they get crushed while in storage.

Wing A

1. From the wing fabric, cut a rectangle 8″ × 11½″ and 2 rectangles 6″ × 8″.

2. Press under ¼″ on an 8″ side of each 6″ × 8″ rectangle.

3. With right sides together, lay the 6″ × 8″ rectangles on top of the larger rectangle so that the folded edges butt up against each other in the center without overlapping. Pin the fabric pieces together.

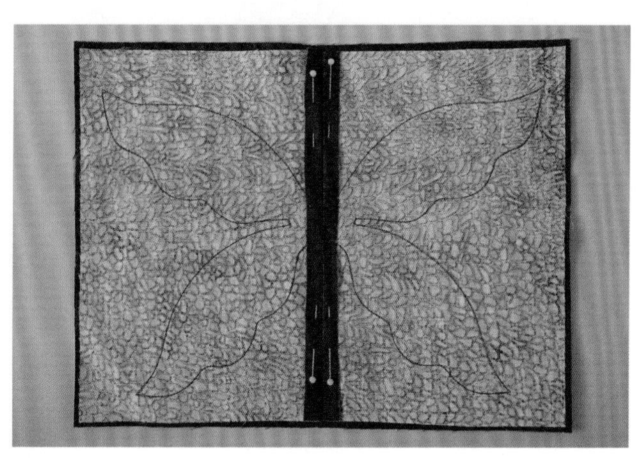

The folded edges create a neat hole, without fraying, for turning the wings right side out and inserting the pipe cleaners.

4. Lay the Wing A template on the fabric, lining up the template's center line where the 2 folded edges meet.

5. Trace the wing on a side of the fabric and then flip the template over to trace it on the other side.

6. Sew around the entire wing piece along the traced line. Cut out the wing, leaving a scant ¼″ seam allowance.

7. Turn the wings right side out through the folded opening in the center. Turning tubes are extremely helpful here. Press.

8. Use a coordinating thread color to sew channels for inserting the pipe cleaners, referring to the template for placement. You can sew the channels freehand or draw them on the fabric with a purple disappearing marker. Sew the lines carefully, keeping the width of each channel ¼″ so the pipe cleaner will slide in easily.

9. Lay the first pipe cleaner on the channel for a length measurement. Fold under both sharp ends ¼″ so they won't poke through the fabric.

10. From the center opening, insert an end of the pipe cleaner into the top left channel and the other end of the pipe cleaner into the top right channel. Go back and forth, inching the pipe cleaner evenly into both wings. Repeat Steps 9 and 10 to insert the second pipe cleaner into the lower channels.

Work back and forth, pushing the pipe cleaner evenly into both wings.

Wing B

Wing B is constructed the same way as Wing A, the only difference being the size and shape of the wings.

1. From the wing fabric, cut a rectangle 5″ × 13½″ and 2 rectangles 5″ × 7″.

2. Press under ¼″ on a 5″ side of each 5″ × 7″ rectangle.

3. With right sides together, lay the 5″ × 7″ rectangles on top of the larger rectangle. The edges that were pressed under should butt up against each other in the center without overlapping. Pin the fabric pieces together.

4. Lay the Wing B template on the fabric so that the template's center line is lined up where the folded edges meet.

5. Trace the wing on a side of the fabric and then flip the template over to trace it on the other side.

6. Follow Steps 6–10 for Wing A. Note that on the Wing B template there is only a single channel for inserting a pipe cleaner.

Attaching the Wings

You can attach the wings now, or you may find it easier to do so after the head and hat are attached to the body. If you prefer to do it later, refer back to this section at that time.

1. Attach the wings before bending and shaping them. Pin Wing A to the center back of the bodice, using the back seam of the bodice as the center line. The hole where you inserted the pipe cleaner will be against the bodice, so it won't show.

2. Sew Wing A to the back, going deep enough to catch the body fabric so that you can be sure the wings are secure. A curved needle is helpful for this. Sew ½″ from the center line on the underside of the wing.

3. Center and pin Wing B on top of Wing A with the open hole facing the bodice so it won't be visible.

4. Sew ¼″ from the center line on the underside of the wing.

5. Gently bend the pipe cleaners to curve the wings, suggesting flight.

Bending the wings gives the illusion of flight.

Making the Head

Follow the instructions in Making the Doll's Head (page 9), Sculpting the Face (page 10), Coloring the Face (page 14), and Adding Eyelids and Lashes (page 17).

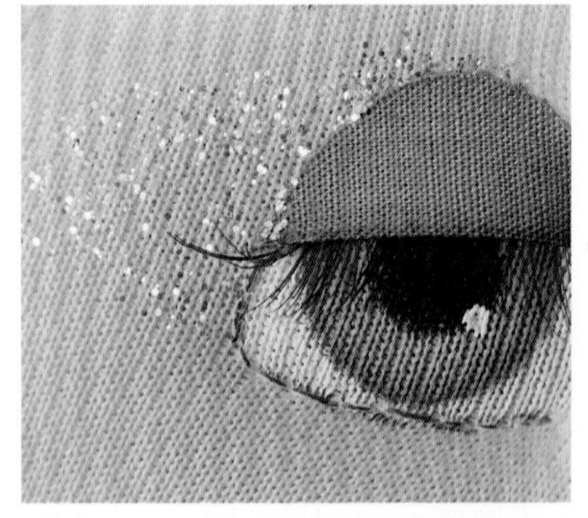

Glitter glue around the outside edge of the eye adds a bit of sparkle.

Making the Ears

1. Trace the Ear template 2 times on doubled fabric. (Use the same cotton fabric that you used to make the body.)

2. Sew on the traced line, using a very short stitch length. Cut out each ear, leaving a ⅛″ seam allowance.

3. Lay the ears on a work surface so that you have a right ear and a left ear facing you. Cut a slit on the back side of each ear, making sure to cut through only a single thickness of fabric. Use tiny turning tubes to turn the ears right side out through the cut.

4. Stuff the ears softly. Push the edges of a small scrap of fabric into the hole on each ear to cover the stuffing.

5. Use a water-soluble fabric marker to draw the line detail of the inside of the ear. Refer to the photos (at right) or create your own details. Sew along the lines, using an open-toe or clear presser foot on your sewing machine; you can also machine stitch free-motion with a darning foot or stitch by hand.

6. Dampen the entire ear using a paintbrush dipped in water. Use the same watercolor pencil colors to shade the ear that you used for the face, rubbing on color with the side of the pencil and then blending it with a paintbrush.

7. Sew a bead or charm to each earlobe as an earring.

8. Fold over the flap so that the top of the ear will roll over at the edge and the tip of the ear will cup slightly and point away from the head. Stitch the flap to the side of the ear, as shown at middle right in the photo.

9. Pin the ears evenly to the head. The bottom of the earlobe should be even with the lips, with the ear positioned over the side seam on the head. Stitch to the head in the center of the ear, leaving the earlobe and the top of the ear unattached.

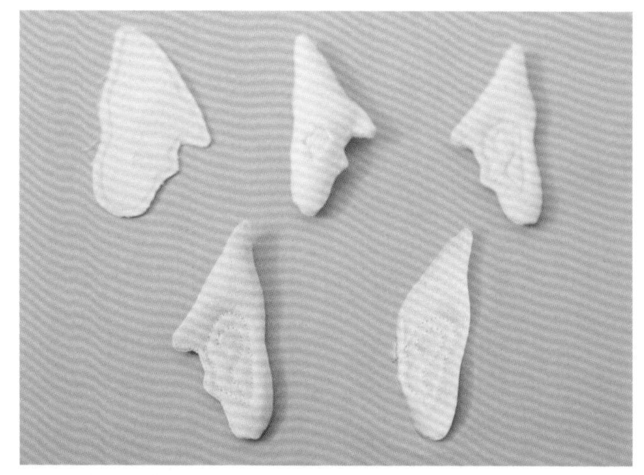

Sew and turn the ears, and then add details with stitching.

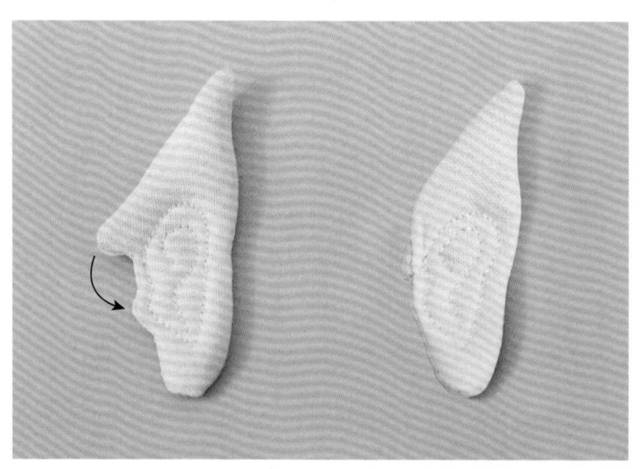

Stitch the flap to the side of the ear, so the ear cups slightly.

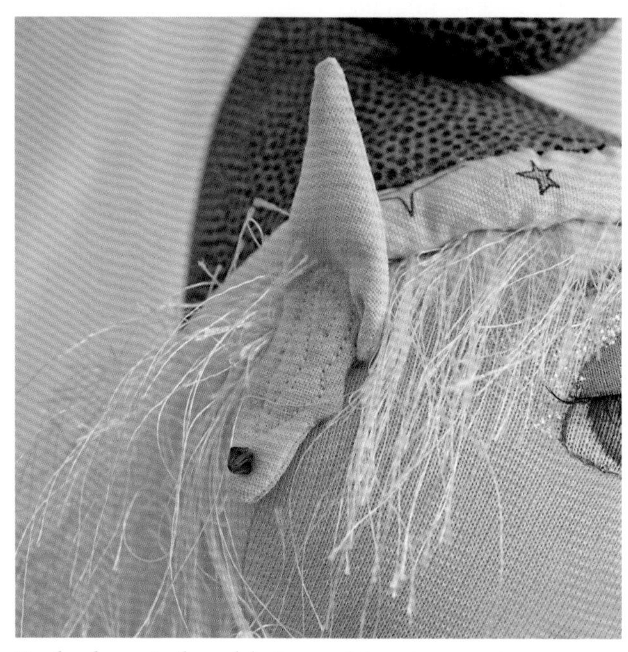

One bead sewn to the earlobe is enough to make an earring.

Attaching the Head

The neck on this doll may seem a bit long, but a long neck will make the head more secure. A head wearing a stuffed hat can be heavy, and a long neck inserted deep into the head will ensure that the head is stable.

1. Push your finger up into the stuffed head to create a hole for inserting the neck. Remove a bit of stuffing if needed. Push the neck firmly up into the opening and pin in place.

2. Use a ladder stitch to join the head and the neck neatly and invisibly, sewing around the base of the head until it is securely attached.

Making the Hat

1. Lay out doubled hat fabric with right sides together. Trace the Hat template onto the wrong side of the fabric.

2. Note the sewing line and the cutting line on the template. Sew around the hat on the (dashed) sewing line.

3. Cut out the hat on the traced (solid) cutting line on the bottom of the hat. Trim along the stitching, leaving a ¼″ seam allowance. Turn right side out.

4. Cut a 2″ × 11″ rectangle from the hat brim fabric. Fold ¼″ under on a 2″ end and press.

5. Fold the brim in half lengthwise, *wrong* sides together, so that it measures 1″ × 11″. Sew along the 11″ length of the brim ¼″ from the raw edges.

6. Softly stuff the brim, pushing in the stuffing with a dowel or a pencil.

7. Pin the brim to the hat with the open ends meeting at the back. To make a neat seam, stick the end with the raw edge into the folded end. Sew the brim to the bottom of the hat.

8. Put a small bit of stuffing into the tip of the hat. Fold a pipe cleaner in half and push the folded end into the tip of the hat, and then stuff the entire hat. Bend the point of the hat to create a nice curve.

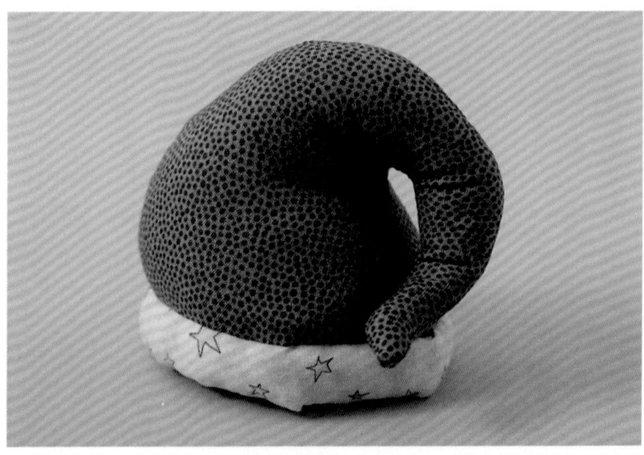

A pipe cleaner in the point helps the hat hold its shape.

Creating a Hairstyle

1. The hat covers much of the head, so there's no need to cover the entire head with hair. Put the hat on the head and use pins to mark the head where the edge of the hat will lie. The hair will be attached inside the circle marked with the pins.

2. Cut several 8″ lengths of eyelash yarn.

3. Pick up 2 or 3 pieces of yarn at a time, fold in half at the center so the bundle is 4″ long, and sew to the head at the fold. The long strands will be trimmed in Step 5. Start sewing on bundles above an ear and

work around the *back* of the head to end above the other ear. Attach the bundles inside the circle of pins marking the hat edge, where the stitching will be covered by the hat.

4 The bangs are made with the eyelash fringe of the yarn. Sew the core of 5 or 6 pieces of yarn from ear to ear across the forehead, making sure it's high enough to be hidden by the hat. Pull the entire fringe down on the forehead to create bangs.

5 Now give the doll a haircut. Even out the length of her hair by cutting off any pieces that hang down too long.

NOTE

When I chose my hair material, I took the same things into consideration as when I chose a durable wing fabric. I decided on eyelash yarn because it will always look good with a simple fluffing. Eyelash yarn has a threadlike fringe and comes in many colors, including multiple colors in a single skein.

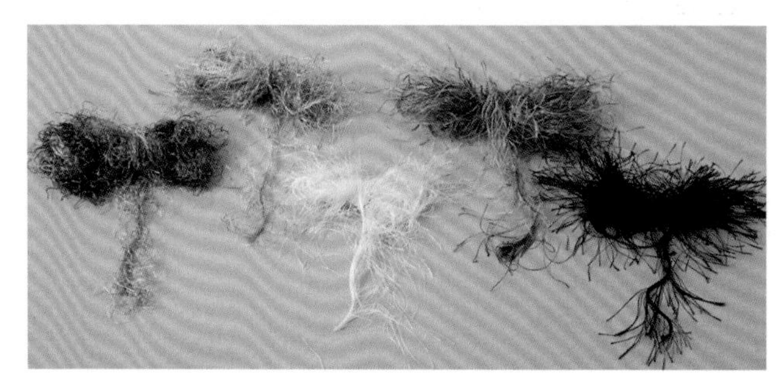

Eyelash yarn

Attaching the Hat

1 Place the hat on the head so that it covers all the attached yarn ends. Pin in place.

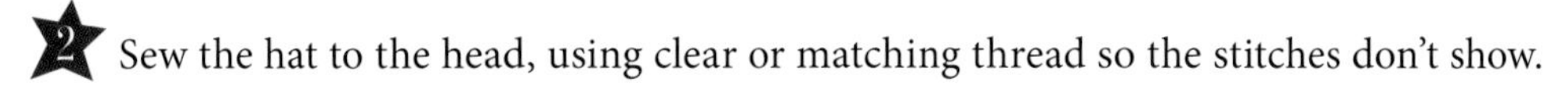

2 Sew the hat to the head, using clear or matching thread so the stitches don't show.

Making the Money Purse

1 With *wrong* sides together, pin together the 4″ × 7″ pieces of fabric for the money purse and lining. Trace the Money Purse template onto the right side of the fabric.

2 Sew a satin stitch on the traced line to join the purse and lining pieces. You can use either matching or contrasting thread.

The Tooth Fairy can put money in the purse and tuck it under a child's pillow.

3 Cut out the purse close to the satin stitching.

4 Fold up the bottom of the purse 2″ with the lining fabric on the inside. Match up the edges and sew the 2″ side seams.

5 Fold the flap over from the top and press.

6 Take the 9″ length of string or ribbon for the purse strap and knot each end. Sew a knotted end to each side of the purse.

Making the Tooth Pouch

1. Using the white tooth pouch fabric, cut 2 squares 3½″ × 3½″ for the outside of the pouch. Also cut 2 squares 3½″ × 3½″ from the pouch lining fabric.

2. With the *wrong* sides together, lay a square of pouch fabric on top of a lining square for the pouch front; repeat for the pouch back. Trace the Tooth Pouch template on the fabric for the pouch front and again on the fabric for the pouch back.

3. There are a number of possibilities for personalizing each child's tooth pouch. You might embroider the child's name in the center of the traced tooth. If your sewing machine embroiders lettering, you can use that feature—or get fancy with some hand embroidery. On the "Emma" pouch (page 20), I wrote the name with a purple disappearing fabric marker and then sewed it with a small zigzag stitch on my machine. The "Anna" pouch (at top right) was decorated with a short satin stitch and variegated thread. Another fun option is to use Lesley Riley's Transfer Artist Paper (see Resources, page 95) to apply a photo of the child, following the package directions.

4. Satin stitch across the top of the tooth, between the marks on the template. Stitch the pouch back and then the pouch front separately.

5. Pin the back to the front, lining sides together, matching up the satin stitching at the top. Satin stitch around the sides and bottom through all 4 thicknesses of fabric.

6. Carefully cut out the tooth close to the satin stitching.

7. Knot each end of the 14″ string or ribbon that will serve as the shoulder strap. Sew a knot to each side of the pouch.

Use thread to add color to the white tooth pouch.

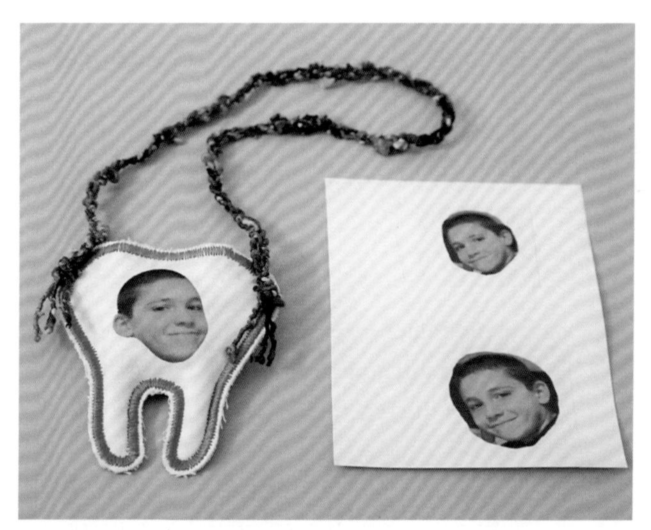

Lesley Riley's Transfer Artist Paper was used to apply photos to plain white cotton fabric for this tooth pouch. If you wish to save your child's baby teeth, the tooth pouch is the perfect place to keep them.

Finishing Touches

Seed beads strung on a thread, alone or with a charm, make a simple but striking necklace for the Tooth Fairy. The charm I used is a heart that reads, "Made with Love." I use this charm on many of my dolls because it seems so appropriate. It's readily available wherever you find beads or jewelry-making supplies.

I often use jump rings (used in jewelry making) as rings for doll fingers. Just open up the ring and slide on a bead. If beads are too small to fit on the jump ring, I simply sew them right onto the finger. Small beads on each side of a larger bead, sewn to the finger with clear thread, create a beautiful ring. Give your doll as many rings as you like.

Most fairies, it seems, carry a wand. In the case of the Tooth Fairy, a toothbrush makes more sense. Why not make it part of the Tooth Fairy tradition to leave a new toothbrush along with the loot in the money purse?

Displaying the Tooth Fairy

The Tooth Fairy isn't meant to be played with. She is posed in the flying position, so hang her where she will be out of the reach of young hands but still very visible.

Sew a jump ring or any small metal or plastic ring to her back below the wings. Make sure the needle goes through the clothes and catches the body fabric. Thread a ribbon or string through the ring for hanging the Tooth Fairy.

Storing the Tooth Fairy

Bringing out the Tooth Fairy only when there's a loose tooth will help to create a tradition that will become a special childhood memory. Store her the same way you care for other treasured holiday decorations. Keep her safe to be handed down to the next generation of children in your family.

Make a keepsake box for your Tooth Fairy. You might copy photos of your children with toothless smiles and decoupage them to the box. You could also include the child's name and the date. Add more photos over the years, and the box will become a pictorial history of the part the Tooth Fairy has played in your family.

All of the time and care you take will ensure that the Tooth Fairy becomes a treasured family heirloom. When your children have children of their own, the Tooth Fairy would be a wonderful gift to pass on to them as new parents.

Tooth Fairy keepsake box

Gallery of Fairies

Princess Nola

The skirt is made from two fabric rectangles 9″ × 18″, gathered at the waist and attached to the body like the Tooth Fairy's slip but with the outer skirt left open in front with the lower corners curved, to reveal the skirt underneath. A small button nose, full eyelids for closed eyes, and puckered lips (for kissing her frog) give Princess Nola a sweet face. Her puckered lips are made by sewing a running stitch in a circle and then pulling the thread to gather it. A stitch across the center gives separation between the lips.

Every princess needs a crown, and beads strung on thin wire allow you to shape Nola's. Embroidery floss is stitched up the back of the bodice and finished with a rosebud. The tiny rubber frog in her hand tells you what every girl knows: "You have to kiss a lot of frogs to find your prince."

Princess Nola was created using the Tooth Fairy pattern. She was made with straight legs (using Template C) so that she can stand, and her arms and hands are positioned differently, but she has the same bodice and sleeves. Princess Nola's right hand is a perfect example of creating expression through hand position.

Housework Fairy

Clara's gloved hands are made from yellow fabric. Her pants use the Pantaloons template with 2″ added to the length and the bottom edges gathered around her legs. Her fleece sweater has darts for a snug fit. Ruffles embellish a classic apron. For the feather duster in her apron pocket, feathers were glued to a dowel and string was wrapped around to cover the quills. Wool curly locks were needle felted to the head and finished with a hair tie.

The base of the stand is painted with black and white acrylic paints in a tile pattern. A hole drilled in the base holds the mop handle, which serves as the doll's support. Natural-colored string forms the head of the mop. The hands were sewn through two tiny holes drilled in the mop handle to secure the doll to the stand.

Clara, the Housework Fairy, is exhausted and catching a quick nap on the job. Clara was made using the Tooth Fairy pattern and the template for Leg C. The body was tilted forward when the legs were attached to allow her to lean on the mop.

The Pincushion Girls

8″ doll

Marigold

This great project gives you an opportunity to try needle felting—or, if you already have needle-felting skills, to be very creative with wool. Warning! The Pincushion Girls are so much fun that you might have to make several of them!

The hat is needle felted and then used as a pincushion (though the entire project actually can be used as a pincushion). The doll is holding a second pincushion that can be made from fabric or needle felted. I designed this pattern to have different sections for keeping my needles in the strawberry separate from my pins in the hat—or you could use them for different pin sizes.

Curly locks wool is used for the hair of all the sample dolls in this chapter, with the exception of Kyah and Stella-Ella (pages 50 and 51), who have synthetic hair. Curly locks are wavy, uncombed, rough wool pieces that have been cut from the fleece, washed, and dyed. I chose this material because it can be handled without messing up the hairstyle. The curly locks are needle felted to the head.

Needle Felting

Needle felting is a dry method of felting wool. A barbed felting needle is repeatedly stabbed into the wool. The barbs on the needle catch the surface scales on the wool fibers, causing them to tangle and interlock. The wool becomes dense and compressed as it's felted.

Shopping for Wool

Wool processing involves carding and combing wool fibers. Carding is a mechanical process that breaks up locks and clumps of fiber, removes short fibers and vegetable matter, and aligns the fibers so they are parallel to each other. The more the wool is carded, the smoother it becomes. Each level of processing means that the wool goes through another session of combing. You can tell the level of processing by the way the wool is labeled.

Curly locks wool has been washed, and often dyed, but it hasn't been carded or combed at all. It has a natural curl that varies depending on the breed of sheep it came from. It's the perfect choice for the hair of a doll that will be handled.

Wool batting has been carded but still has fibers going in every direction. The fibers aren't parallel, so the wool is in the beginning stages of felting. This means that the fiber will felt without much effort. Wool batting is perfect for making the hats for the Pincushion Girls.

Wool sliver has been removed from the carding drum in long, uniform widths, whereas batting has been removed in big sheets. Sliver may also be called *pencil roving,* a reference to the shape (long, slender ropes of wool).

Wool roving is processed (combed) more than either batting or sliver. It may be given a twist in preparation for making yarn. It takes more effort to felt at this point because the fibers are well aligned. However, it does make great doll hair and eyebrows.

Wool top is very smooth and fine, with all the fibers going in the same direction. All the short fibers have been removed, so it doesn't look hairy, and the natural crimp has been straightened out. Wool top is better suited to wet felting than to dry needle felting. You would need to spend a fair amount of time "messing it up" to get it ready for needle felting. It makes great doll hair.

Consider the Source

Different breeds of sheep produce wool with different properties. Merino wool is known for its softness and is often compared to cashmere, making it highly sought after. There are many other breeds, but the important thing to know is that each breed's wool displays its own distinct fiber qualities—length, crimp, coarseness, and so on. After working with different fibers you will become familiar with their specific characteristics.

Materials

See page 8 for lists of general sewing and doll-making equipment.

- ¼ yard cotton fabric for body (Use Kona Cotton or another fabric with a high thread count; thinner muslins do not work well for tiny body parts.)
- 15″ × 15″ cotton fabric for blouse
- 3″ × 4″ white cotton fabric for eyes
- 1½″ × 4″ solid or print cotton fabric for eyelids
- 1½″ × 4″ fusible web for eyelids
- 2 solid-color ½″ buttons for eyes
- 2 tiny beads or ¼″ black buttons for pupils of eyes
- Beads for jewelry (It takes a 2″ string of beads for a bracelet, a 3½″–4″ string for a necklace, and 1–3 beads for a ring.)
- 4″–5″ wood base (found in the wood section of the craft store)
- Acrylic paint for wood base (your choice of color)
- 4″ × 12″ red cotton for tomato (*optional*)
- 4″ × 7″ print cotton for strawberry (*optional*)
- 3″ × 3″ scrap of green felt for tomato or strawberry leaf (*optional*)
- Fabric paint for fingernails (or textile medium added to acrylic paint)
- Artist-quality watercolor pencils for lips and cheeks
- 2 ounces wool batting for needle felting hat
- ½ ounce curly locks wool for hair
- #40 (fine) felting needle
- 2″-thick dense foam for needle-felting work surface (Purchase the type used for chair padding—usually green but also found in black and white. The denser the foam, the longer it will stand up to the repeated poking of the felting needle.)
- Polyester fiberfill
- White craft glue
- Tiny turning tubes (*optional* but helpful)
- Doll needle at least 3″ long
- Quilting thread

Templates Required

You'll use the following templates (pages 84–86) for a Pincushion Girl:

Head Front, Head Back, Ear, Arm, Body Back, Body Front Bust, Body Front Torso, Body Base, Blouse Front, Blouse Back, Blouse Sleeve, Small Eye Button Cover, Large Eye Button Cover, Hat Brim; choose either Tomato and Tomato Leaf or Strawberry and Strawberry Leaf

All templates are traced onto 2 layers of fabric placed right sides together, unless otherwise indicated.

Constructing the Body

1. On a single thickness of body fabric, trace the Body Front Bust, Body Front Torso, Body Back, and Body Base templates.

2. Cut out each piece on the traced line.

3. Sew the front bust to the front torso at the breast line.

4. With right sides together, pin the front to the back. Sew down each side of the body, leaving the neck and bottom of the torso open.

5. With right sides together, pin the body base to the bottom of the torso and sew.

6. Turn the body right side out through the neck. Turning tubes are helpful for this task.

7. Stuff the body firmly with fiberfill and whipstitch the neck closed.

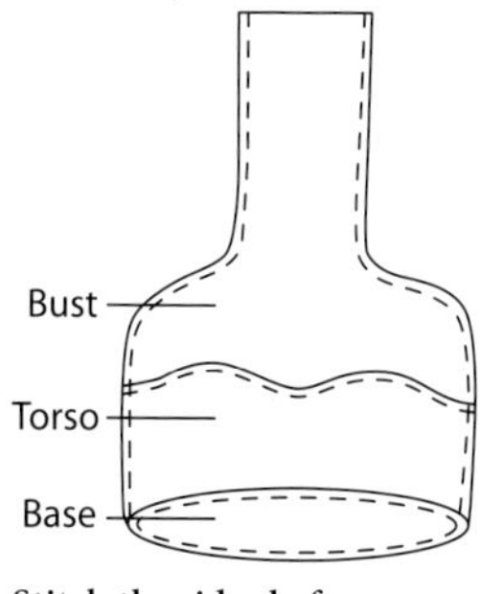

Stitch the sides before you attach the body base.

Making the Head, Arms, and Ears

Use the trace-sew-cut method to make the doll's head, arms, and ears.

1. Note the arrows on the templates showing the direction of stretch in the fabric. On doubled fabric, lay out and trace the Head Front, Head Back, Arm (trace twice), and Ear (trace twice) templates.

2. Sew around the ears and arms, using a short stitch length and leaving the pieces open at the tabs for turning and stuffing.

3. Sew the nose side of the head front. On the head back, sew the side with the neck opening, referring to the template to confirm stitching and cutting lines.

4. Cut out the ears and arms, leaving a ⅛″ seam allowance. Turn right side out.

5. Cut out the head front and back, leaving a ⅛″ seam allowance on the stitched side and cutting directly on the marked tracing line on the unstitched side.

Finishing the Arms

Sewing the lines between the fingers will be easier if you use a disappearing fabric marker to mark them first, as shown on the template. It's also helpful to mark the top of the palm so you can see clearly where to stop each line of stitching.

Mark the finger lines and the top of the palm where the fingers end.

You can stitch the lines either before or after the hand is stuffed. However, if you sew first and then stuff each finger individually, the lines will be deeper and the fingers will be rounder, giving a neater appearance. (The solid rod from the set of tiny turning tubes will fit in the tiny fingers for stuffing them.)

After you've stitched and stuffed the fingers, stuff the rest of the arm and then close the stuffing hole with a ladder stitch.

Tip *As an alternative, you can create the look of gloved hands for your Pincushion Girl. Refer to Making the Arms for the Tiny Flower Fairy* *(page 69)**. Join white fabric for the gloves to the body fabric and then trace the Arm template onto the sewn fabric. Leave as is or add a trim over the seam.*

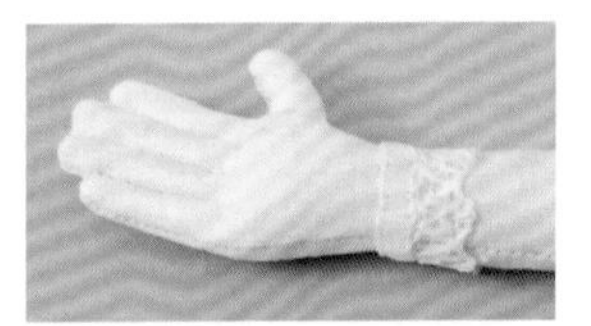

Use white fabric for the "glove" portion of the hand.

Painting the Fingernails

It's easiest to paint the fingernails before the arms are attached to the body. Lay the arms on a work surface so that you have right and left hands. You can use fabric paint for the nails, or you can add a textile medium to acrylic paint you have on hand. A dime-size drop of paint is more than enough.

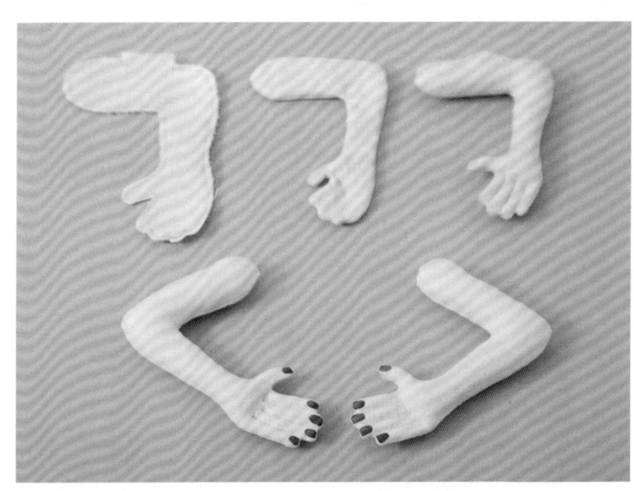

Stitch and stuff the arms, and then paint the fingernails as the finishing touch.

Finishing the Head

1. With right sides together, pin the head front to the head back. Use many pins so that you *do not* ease the fabric as you sew.

2. Sew the head front to the head back.

3. Turn right side out and stuff firmly.

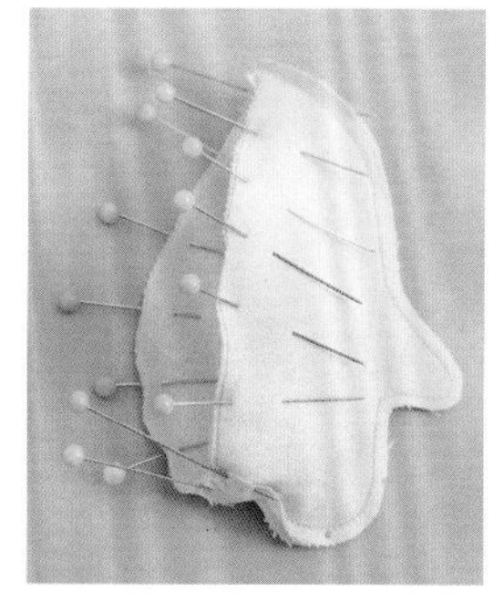

Use a lot of pins to keep the fabric from shifting.

Creating the Face

Sculpt the doll's face with a strong quilting thread (matching the thread color to the fabric as closely as possible) and a 3″ or longer needle that will reach from the back of the head to the face. Sew with a long length of thread. If you run out of thread, knot the thread at the back of the head and begin a new length. Always start and stop at the back of the head. The hair will hide the knots.

1. Use a disappearing or water-soluble fabric marker to draw a line down each side of the nose, from the bridge of the nose to the top of the nostril. The lines should be the same distance from the center seam.

2. Outline the nostrils on each side of the nose. The lines I've drawn on the sample head in the photo (at right) may seem a bit large, but once the nose is sculpted, the size is just perfect.

3. Knot the thread on the seam at the back of the head and come out on a line on the bridge of the nose. Sew on the lines back and forth (side to side), from the top of the nose to the top of the nostrils, with consistently tiny stitches.

4. When you reach the nostril, the stitch direction will change to up and down. When you finish a nostril, bring the needle out at the top of the opposite nostril, and stitch up and down with tiny stitches. Finish the nose by knotting the thread at the back of the head. See Sculpting the Nose (page 12) for more guidance.

5. Use the center seam of the face as the mark for the center of the lips. Sculpt a stitch or 2 on each side of the center seam, depending on how wide you want the smile to be. After each stitch, bring the thread to the back of the head and knot it.

Draw sculpting lines with a disappearing fabric marker (*top*); sculpt the nose and mouth (*left*); color the cheeks and lips (*right*); and then add the eyebrows, lashes, and button eyes.

Coloring the Cheeks and Lips

1 Use a paintbrush and clean water to wet the whole face, just past the side seams.

2 Use the side of a watercolor pencil to rub color onto the cheeks. Blend with a paintbrush. The color will appear a bit lighter after it dries.

3 Use the center seam of the face as the center of the lips; the sculpting stitches you made for the mouth mark the separation between the lips. Outline the lips and then fill in with color. You can use a single color or outline with a dark color and fill in with a lighter shade of the same color. For more detailed instructions, refer to Coloring the Lips (page 16).

Making the Button Eyes

The shape and size of the button you choose for the eyes will give your Pincushion Girl her own personality. *If you use buttons with a shank,* you'll need to poke a hole in the face fabric so the shank will go through and let the button lie flat on the face. *If you use buttons with holes,* you'll need to tie on quilting thread for attaching to the head later, since you won't have access to the holes once the eye fabric covers the button. Thread a 20″ piece of quilting thread through the button holes so the 10″ thread tails hang from the back of the button. The thread tails need to be long enough to reach from the eye to the back of the head.

1 Iron fusible web to the back of the 1½″ × 4″ eyelid fabric. Cut a little off a 4″ side to be certain that the fusible web goes all the way to the edge of the fabric, ensuring that it won't fray later.

2 Fuse the eyelid fabric to the 3″ × 4″ white eye fabric, as shown.

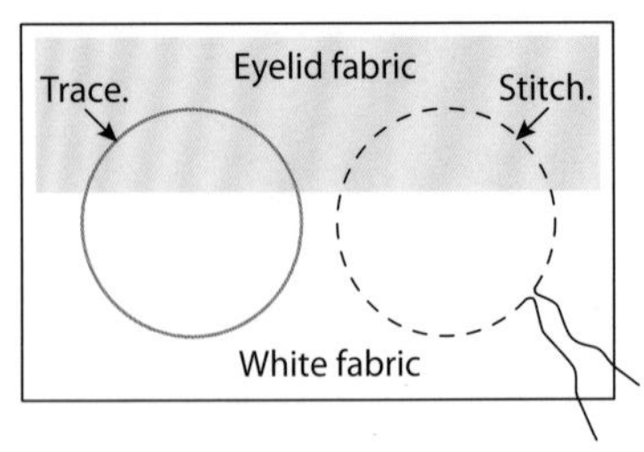

Make the white of the eye larger than the eyelid.

3 The eye fabric will be gathered around the eye button. For round buttons, I find that in most cases a thread spool makes the perfect-size pattern for the eyes. Alternatively, use the Small or Large Eye Button Cover template pattern (page 86). Use a pencil to mark the fabric, placing the template so the eyelid portion is a bit smaller than the white of the eye. If the eyelid is too big, the doll will look sleepy. Use quilting thread to make a running stitch directly on the pencil line.

4 Cut out each eye ⅛″ outside the running stitch. Stitching before you cut minimizes fraying.

5 Place the eye button in the center of the fabric circle and pull the thread of the running stitch to gather the fabric around the button. Secure the thread. If the back seems too bulky, press with a hot iron to flatten the gathers.

6 Using black thread, sew on a black button, bead, or snap for the pupil of the eye. Tie with a knot.

Attaching the Eyes

To attach the button eyes, use the quilting thread you tied onto the buttons earlier if they have holes, or tie on thread now if your buttons have shanks. Use a 3″ or longer needle so you can go in at the eye and come out next to the seam at the back of the head. Repeat for the second eye, bringing the thread out on the other side of the seam.

Pull both sets of eye threads to determine if the eyes are even. If necessary, pull off an eye button and reposition it. When the eyes are even, tie the thread of an eye to the thread of the other eye at the back of the head, tight enough so the buttons are held firmly against the face. Tying the eye buttons together lets you move them slightly to adjust if an eye is loose.

Stitching Brows and Lashes

The eyebrows and eyelashes are stitched with a single strand of sewing thread. You can use black, brown, red—it's your choice. Thread a 3″ or longer needle with a long length of thread. Knot at the seam on the back of the head and come out next to the eye where you want the lashes to be. Slide the needle off the thread and replace it with a shorter, more manageable needle.

When you finish stitching the lashes on the first eye, bring the needle up to the brow and stitch the brow. The shape of the eyebrow will help to define the doll's look.

Repeat the process for the second eye. If you make a stitch that's out of place, simply pull it out. When you are finished, use the longer needle to bring the thread to the back of the head and knot it. The hair will cover all the knots in the back.

The shape of the eye buttons, the color of the eyelid fabric, and the size and placement of the pupils give each face its own look.

Attaching the Ears and Arms

1. Turn the ears right side out. Tuck the tabs into the stuffing hole.

2. Stuff the ears with fiberfill. Use a ladder stitch to close the stuffing hole.

3. Lay the ears out in front of you so that you have a right ear and a left ear. Sew an earring to each earlobe, knotting the thread on the back of the lobe. The earrings can be a single bead, button, or charm, or they can be several beads strung together.

4. Pin an ear to each side seam of the head so they are even with each other. The seam of the ear will lie on the side seam of the head. Sew the ears to the head, stitching so they will stick out. Knot the thread behind the ear, where the knot will be hidden.

5. Pin the arms to the body at the shoulder. Position the hands to allow them to hold a pincushion later.

6. Sew the arms to the body.

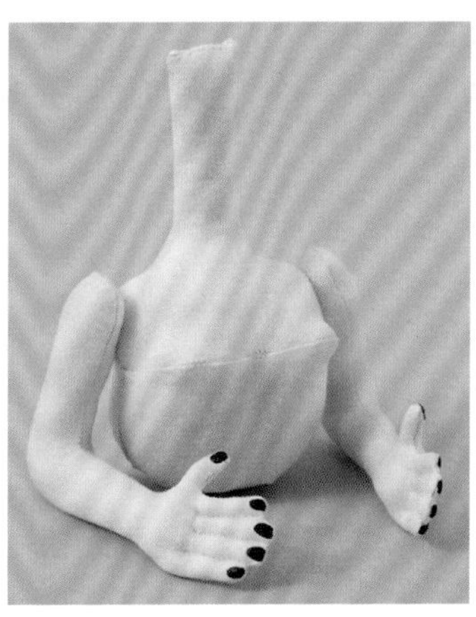

Position the doll's hands to hold her pincushion.

Making the Blouse

1 Lay out the Blouse templates on the blouse material. Trace the Blouse Back template onto a single layer of fabric. Trace the Blouse Front and Sleeve templates onto doubled fabric. Cut out pieces.

2 With right sides together, sew the front to the back at the shoulders. Turn under the raw edge ¼″ around the neckline and front of the blouse. Topstitch in place, or use a decorative stitch with contrasting thread. Add decorative trim or iron-on thread, if you wish.

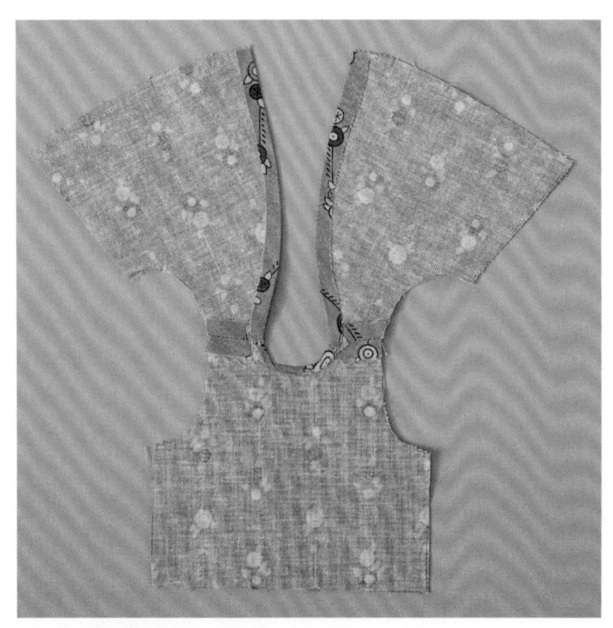

Turn under the edge along the front and neckline.

Tip *Iron-on thread (see Resources, page 95) is a fusible embellishment that is fun and easy to use. Just place the thread where you want it, cover with a Teflon pressing cloth (included with the thread), and press to adhere. It can be used on fabric or paper, and you can embellish it further by sewing over it after it has been fused. Iron-on thread comes in different widths and colors, even with glitter.*

The sample doll has red iron-on thread as an added detail along the neck, front, and sleeves of the blouse. Iron the thread to the blouse before you sew on the sleeves. This will allow the fabric to lie flat for pressing.

3 Referring to the template pattern for placement, sew a dart on each side of the blouse front.

4 Add trim to the bottom edge of the sleeves ½″ above the lower edge, if you wish. Sew a gathering stitch at the top and bottom of each sleeve as indicated on the template pattern.

5 Pull the thread to gather the top of the sleeve. With right sides together, pin the sleeve to the armhole opening on the blouse. Sew the sleeve to the blouse.

6 Sew the underside of the sleeve and the side of the blouse in a single continuous seam.

7 Sew a gathering stitch around the bottom edge of the blouse.

8 Put the blouse on the doll and ladder stitch the front opening closed.

9 Pull the thread to gather the bottom of the blouse under the doll's body; arrange the gathers evenly. Before cutting the thread, stitch the blouse to the underside of the body. Tacking the blouse to the body will make the body more secure when the bottom is glued to the base.

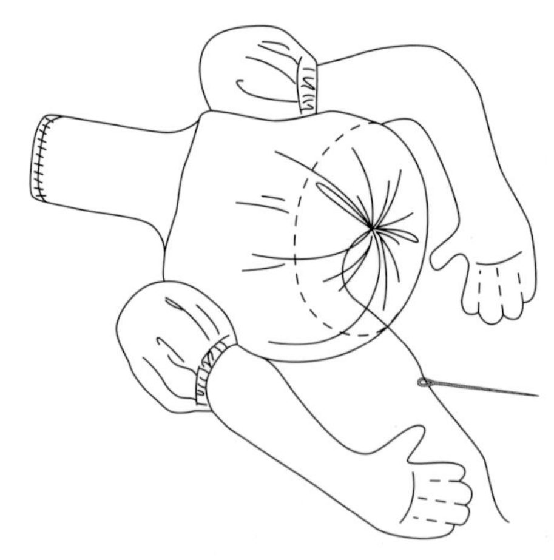

Gather the edge of the blouse under the torso. Rub the torso bottom on a hot iron to flatten the gathers and make a smooth area for attaching to the base.

10 Gather the lower edge of each sleeve and knot the thread.

Embellishing with Jewelry

You can add rings, a necklace, and a bracelet either now or later. I prefer to add them at this point, since the body is easiest to handle before the head and base are attached.

A few beads will go a long way on this tiny body. One to three beads are plenty to make a ring. Sew the beads to the finger, knotting on the palm side of the finger. Keep it simple, or make it elaborate and have fun with it.

Finishing the Head

Push the neck firmly up into the opening in the head and pin in place. Use a ladder stitch to sew around the base of the head until it is securely attached.

Needle Felting the Hat

1. For the top part of Marigold's hat, pull off a few pieces of wool batting and start to roll the wool into a ball, stabbing with the felting needle as you go. Keep adding wool until you have a hat top the right size for your doll.

The more you stab with the needle, the firmer the wool will become as it is felted. Shallow stabs at a 45° angle will clean up the hairy surface of the hat.

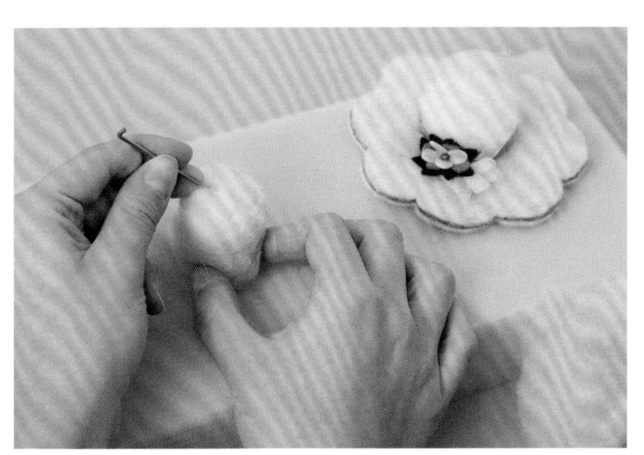

Stab at a 45° angle to smooth the surface.

2. For the brim, tear off several pieces of wool batting and stack in a circle, using the Hat Brim template pattern as guide. As you stack the fibers to fill the circle, alternate the direction of the fibers. Your stack should be 1″–1½″ tall initially. Needle felt the fibers together to form the disk shape. For any area that seems too thin, simply pull off another piece of wool batting and felt it on. Fold the edges under and felt in place to create a circular shape of uniform thickness.

3. Set the top of the hat on the center of the brim and needle felt them together.

4. Needle felt a large dent on the underside of the hat so it will sit nicely on the doll's head.

5. Embellish the hat with colored wool, ribbons, buttons, charms, or flowers.

The fabric design of each doll's blouse was copied and needle felted onto the hat.

Attaching the Hair and Hat

1. Try the hat on the doll's head—you won't need to put hair where the hat covers the head.

2. Arrange the wool curly locks on the head, needle felting each piece of wool onto the head as you add it. Save the best curls to go around the face. A few pokes here and there will hold the hair in place. Be careful not to continually poke the needle in the same spot, or you will make a hole in the fabric.

3. Position the hat on the head and pin it in place. Since the hat will be used as a pincushion, it needs to be very secure on the head. Use a 3″ or 5″ needle so you can sew through the hat and head in a single stitch. Use a curved needle, if you prefer, with matching or clear thread.

Sew all the way around the underside of the hat, catching the head fabric with each stitch, until the hat feels secure. Hide the stitches under embellishments where you can. If a stitch leaves a dent in the wool, use a pin to pull or fluff out the wool, or fill in the dent with more wool.

Making the Doll's Pincushion

Included with this pattern are templates for both a strawberry and a tomato pincushion. Use one or the other, or you can take this opportunity to continue with whatever theme you have chosen for *your* Pincushion Girl. Look at the sample dolls (pages 50 and 51) for inspiration, and pull out that artistic license of yours.

Strawberry Pincushion

1. Use the Strawberry template to cut a strawberry shape from fabric. Fold in half with right sides together and sew along the straight edges.

2. Sew a gathering stitch around the top opening.

3. Turn right side out and stuff firmly. Pull the threads of the gathering stitch and secure.

4. Cut a strawberry leaf from green felt. Glue or sew the leaf to the top of the strawberry.

5. Sew the hands of the doll to the sides of the strawberry.

You can be creative with the pincushion the doll holds. Choose something that adds to the theme of your project.

Tomato Pincushion

1. Use the Tomato template to cut 6 tomato pieces from fabric.

2. With right sides together, sew the pieces together side by side with a scant ¼″ seam allowance. Sew the first piece to the last one, leaving a hole at the top for turning and stuffing.

3. Turn right side out and stuff firmly.

4. Cut a leaf from green felt. Glue or sew the leaf to the top of the tomato.

5. Sew the doll's hands to the sides of the tomato.

Adding the Base

1 Pincushion Girls are glued to 4″ or 5″ wood cutouts. Paint the wood base with acrylic paint in the color of your choice.

2 The doll is glued to the base with white craft glue. Put a generous amount of glue on the underside of the body and the pincushion the doll is holding. Position the doll on the base, and then stretch a rubber band around each shoulder and the base to hold everything in place while the glue dries. Let the doll sit overnight to let the glue dry completely.

Edgar

Tip *As an alternative to a wood cutout, you could select a small papier-mâché box as the base for your Pincushion Girl. The box can then be used to store extra pins and needles. Paint or decoupage the box with images or objects in keeping with the doll's theme. Edgar's box was decorated with acrylic paint and sealed with a clear spray-on acrylic coating. Attach the doll to the box lid the same as for a wood base.*

Gallery of Pincushion Girls

Willa is holding a needle-felted spool of thread inspired by her blouse fabric. Her eyes started with buttons that were covered in white fabric. Pink fabric was fused over half of each button to create eyelids, and 4mm black button "pupils" finished the eyes.

Choose a hair color that will complement the overall look of the doll. It can be fun to choose something unexpected. Sosie's hair is curly locks wool that has been dyed green. She is holding a heart pincushion with hand-stitched edge detail.

A beret is a simple but effective shape for a hat. Kyah's synthetic black braids are stitched to the top of her head under the beret. Cutting the braids in different lengths gives the hairstyle some fullness.

Midge's pillbox hat fits her personality perfectly. Her hair is tied up in a tidy bun, and she's wearing her best pearls. Her 2½″-wide eyeglasses help her find the needles in her needle-felted purse.

Stella-Ella's teardrop-shaped button eyes add expression to her face. Synthetic kinked hair is sewn to her head. Buttons embellish her needle-felted hat and complement the button-themed fabric used for her blouse.

Beatrice's black-and-white theme was inspired by the sewing-notion print fabric used for her blouse. Her square button eyes come to life with black snaps sewn to the centers. Red lips and fingernails add just a splash of color.

The circle print in Glady's blouse is carried through in her needle-felted hat. Small bits of colored felt were used to add the blouse design to a hat made from core wool.

Leonie's hair is the natural color it was when the wool came off the sheep. The tiny, tight curls are the perfect size for this doll. Black ¼″ buttons are tied to the white of the eye, and the eyelids are the same color as the face. A decorative stitch on the blouse is a subtle yet effective embellishment.

Lyle the Elf

14″ sitting doll

I created this pattern because I felt it had the potential to become a much-loved family heirloom. I will admit that creating a Santa crossed my mind, too—but just briefly. Everyone knows Santa, and we all recognize the big guy in the red suit. But elves are more fun, because you can use your artistic license to implement your own interpretation.

We don't have quite the same preconceived expectations of elves that we do of Santa. The look of the face, the colors of the fabrics, the design of the outfit, and even the gender are up to you. You can create several elves, each with its own personality, so that everyone gets an heirloom to treasure.

You aren't limited to a red-and-green palette. Chances are you will be working on this project long before the Christmas-themed fabrics are on the shelves of the fabric store. If you have seasonal prints in your fabric stash, you can work with those, but don't feel that any of your fabric choices need to have a Christmas theme. The pointed ears and pointed shoes will let everyone know that this doll is an elf. I gave each elf the same twisted hat so they would look like they'd all come from the same North Pole.

There are so many jobs at the North Pole that it will be easy to personalize each elf for its lucky recipient. We all know that the elves make toys, but keep in mind that there's an entire community to run! There's head of security, elf on reindeer stable duty, mail room elf, administrator of the naughty-and-nice list, sleigh mechanic, spreader of cheer with song and dance—just to name a few. All these occupations offer creative opportunities for personalizing your own crew of elves and making them worthy of being passed down to the next generation of your family.

Materials

See page 8 for lists of general sewing and doll-making equipment.

- ⅓ yard cotton fabric with small stripes for body, legs, and arms
- 12″ × 14″ flesh-tone polyester knit for head, eyelids, and ears
- ¼ yard (or 1 fat quarter) cotton print fabric for hat (actual required size 9″ × 14″)
- 2½″ × 12″ cotton print fabric for hat band
- 2½″ × 16″ cotton print fabric for scarf
- 8″ × 11″ cotton print fabric for gloves
- ¼ yard cotton print fabric for shirt
- 7″ × 10″ cotton print fabric for shirt collar
- ¼ yard cotton print fabric for pants
- 2″ × 17″ cotton print fabric for belt
- 6″ × 12″ vinyl or imitation leather for shoes
- 2″ × 5″ synthetic fur or felt for shoe trim
- ¾″ or 1″ buckle for belt (available in the scrapbooking department of the craft store)
- 3 jingle bells (½″) for hat and shoes
- 5 jingle bells (¼″) for shirt collar
- 5 buttons (⅛″ or ¼″) for shirt
- 2 or 4 buttons (⅛″ or ¼″) for gloves
- 1 skein embroidery floss for scarf fringe
- 2″ × 4″ scrap of fusible web for eyelids
- ¼ skein wool yarn for hair and eyebrows (*alternatives:* 1 small bag synthetic curly hair *or* ½ ounce wool roving)
- #40 (fine) felting needle
- 2 white pipe cleaners for fingers
- Polyester fiberfill
- Coordinating thread for sewing
- Strong quilting thread for sculpting face (to match face fabric)
- Artist-quality watercolor pencils for coloring face

Tip *You may want to include props for your elf—store-bought items, found objects, or pieces made by you—to help personalize him or her.*

NOTE

The Christmas present on which the elf sits is a cardboard box covered with fabric. The amount of fabric you need depends on the size of the box you use—any box can be recycled to use as a present. The bow for Lyle's present requires a 6″ × 16″ piece of print cotton fabric, plus what's wrapped around the box. The bow fabric wrapped around the box is 1″ wide.

Templates Required

You'll use the following templates (pages 87–92) for Lyle the Elf:

Head Front, Head Back, Ear, Eye, Eyelid, Gloves, Glove Band, Arm, Leg, Body Back, Body Front, Hat, Hat Band, Scarf, Shirt Front, Shirt Back, Shirt Sleeve, Shirt Collar, Belt, Pants Front, Pants Back, Shoe, Shoe Sole, Shoe Toe, Shoe Trim, Present Bow, Present Bow Tie

All templates are traced onto 2 layers of fabric placed right sides together, unless otherwise indicated.

Constructing the Body

An arrow on the Body Front, Body Back, Arm, and Leg templates indicates the direction of the stripe in the fabric. When you are working with a striped print, it's important to take the time to line up the stripes when you join the pieces. Keep this in mind as you cut out the body pieces, and line up the stripes as you pin the fabric together.

1. Using the Body Front and Body Back templates, cut 2 of each shape.

2. With right sides together, sew the fronts together at the center front.

3. With right sides together, sew the backs together at the center back.

4. With right sides together, pin the front to the back. Stitch, leaving the neck open for turning and stuffing.

5. Turn the body right side out and stuff firmly. Whipstitch the neck closed.

Making the Arms and Legs

1. Trace, stitch, and stuff the arms and wired hands/gloves according to the directions in Creating Arms and Hands (pages 17–19).

2. Trace the Leg template 2 times on the wrong side of doubled fabric. If you are using a striped fabric, take the time to line up the stripes and pin the fabric before sewing.

3. Sew each leg on the traced line, leaving it open at the tab for turning and stuffing. Trim the stitching, leaving a ⅛″ seam allowance. Cut the tab directly on the solid cutting line.

4. Turn each leg right side out. Stuff firmly. Tuck the tabs inside the stuffing holes and ladder stitch the openings closed.

Assembling the Body

1. Pin the legs to the body in the sitting position. The base of the body and the underside of both legs should all be touching the sitting surface.

2. Ladder stitch each leg to the body.

3. Pin the arms to the shoulders. Consider what you may put in the doll's hands as you position the arms.

4. Ladder stitch each arm to the body.

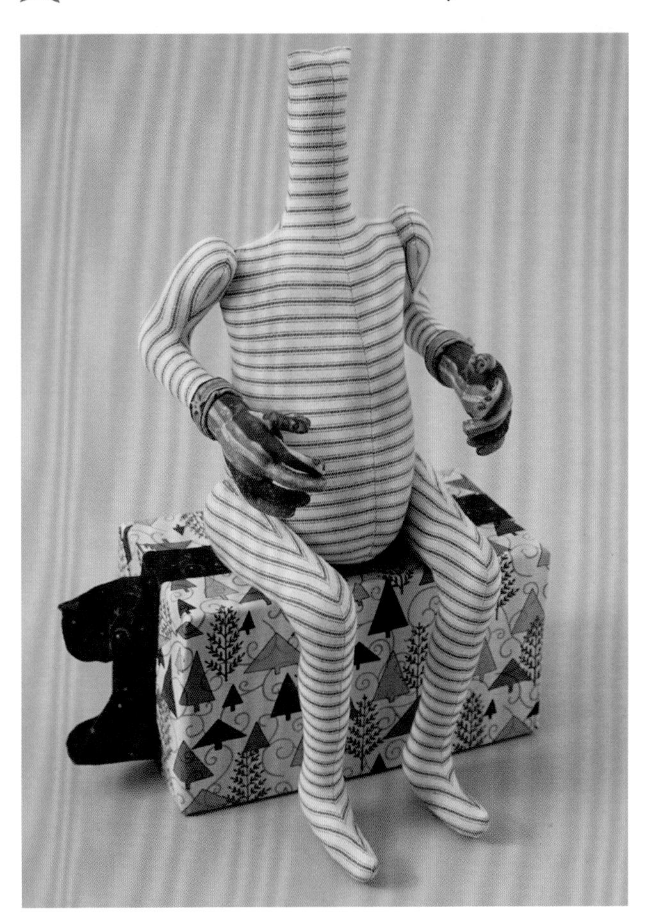

Think about what will be in the hands and position the arms accordingly.

Dressing the Doll

Shirt

1 Trace the Shirt Collar template on the wrong side of doubled fabric.

2 Sew on the traced line, leaving the collar open as shown by the solid line on the template pattern.

3 Cut out the collar, leaving a ⅛″ seam allowance. Where you left the neck unsewn, cut directly on the line.

4 Turn the collar right side out and press. Sew a ¼″ jingle bell to each of the 5 points on the collar, add decoration to the back flap of the collar, or do both.

5 Use the templates to cut 1 shirt back, 2 shirt fronts, and 2 sleeve pieces.

6 With right sides together, sew the front to the back at the shoulders.

7 With right sides together, pin the sleeve to the shirt armhole. Sew.

8 With right sides together, pin the underside of the sleeves and the side seams of the shirt (shirt back to shirt front). Sew each sleeve and side in a single continuous seam.

9 Turn the shirt right side out and press. Put the shirt on the body. Turn under the raw edge on a side of the front opening so it lies on the body's center line; finger-press or pin the fold. Use a disappearing fabric marker to mark where the shirt fronts meet. This will help you to position the collar.

10 While the shirt is still on the body, fit the sleeve for length. You can hem the sleeve or roll it up into a cuff. Make the sleeve short enough that it doesn't cover the glove.

11 Remove the shirt. Press the fold in the shirt front center and also the sleeve hem (or cuff).

12 Sew the sleeve hems. If you choose to make a rolled-up cuff, press the cuff in place.

13 Pin the underside of the collar to the shirt neckline, using the fold and mark you made when trying on the shirt to position the collar. Sew the underside of the collar to the shirt with a ⅛″ seam allowance. Fold under the raw edge of the upper side to meet the seam you've just sewn. Whipstitch in place around the neckline. Press the collar.

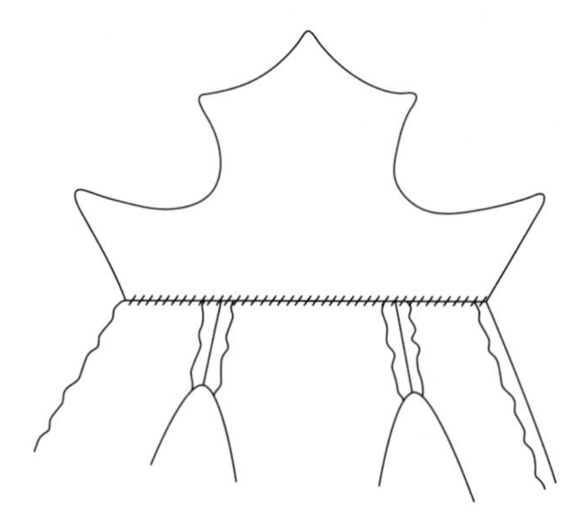

Attaching the collar

14 Sew 5 buttons to the folded front edge of the shirt, keeping in mind that only about 3″ of the shirt front will show once the pants are on. Evenly space the buttons within this area.

15 Place the shirt on the body. Overlap the front edges slightly with the button edge on top. Ladder stitch the front of the shirt.

Tip *When I make a blouse or shirt that will be tucked in, I tack the bottom edge to the body. This helps keep the shirt tucked in when the pants are put on. Line up the side seam of the shirt with the side seam of the body and make a stitch to anchor the shirt to the body. I also make a stitch at the center back and again at the center front. Since the shirt will be tucked in, there's no need to hem the bottom edge.*

Pants

1 Use the Pants Front and Pants Back templates to cut 2 of each shape.

2 With right sides together, sew the center seam to join the 2 front pieces. With right sides together, sew the center seam to join the 2 back pieces, starting at the dot on the template.

3 With right sides together, pin the front to the back at the sides and inseam. Sew down each side of the pants. Sew the inseam.

4 Hem the pants legs, so they rest just above the knee (approximately ½″ hem).

5 Turn the pants right side out, press, and put them on the doll.

6 Fold under the pants waist about ½″ and stick pins through the pants and into the doll body to hold in place. Fold under each side of the back opening ¼″ so the sides meet at the center back. The pants waist should fit without gathers.

7 Use a ladder stitch to close the back opening of the pants.

Belt

The measurements for the belt will depend on the belt buckle that you use. The sample project uses a ¾″ belt buckle with a ½″ opening, so the belt is ½″ wide to accommodate this buckle. The finished belt length is 14″.

Determine the size of the opening in your buckle and adjust the belt width as needed. The buckle size won't alter the length of the belt.

1 Use the Belt template to cut out the belt on the fold, as indicated on the template. If you need to adjust the belt to accommodate your buckle, do that now.

2 With right sides together, fold the belt in half lengthwise. Using a ¼″ seam allowance, sew across an end of the belt and down the length, stopping in the middle. Then sew across the other end of the belt and down the length, stopping about 1″ before you meet the opposite stitches.

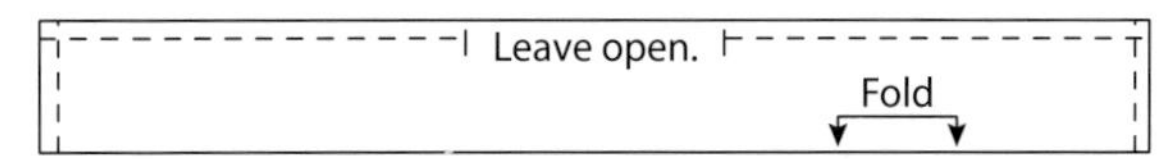

The belt can be turned right side out quickly with turning tubes.

3 Turn the belt right side out through the hole you left in the center, using turning tubes. Press.

4 Loop an end around the buckle's center bar to the inside of the belt; stitch in place.

5 Place the belt around the waist of the pants, loop the free end through the buckle, and tighten.

6 Using matching thread, sew with small, hidden stitches at the edge of the belt all the way around to hold it in place.

Sew the belt to the body to keep it securely in place.

Tip *If you prefer, you can dress the doll in suspenders instead of a belt. Follow Steps 1–3 to make 2 belts, each 9″ long. Attach these to the front and back of the pants with small buttons. Another option is to slide a buckle onto each suspender, positioned just below the shoulder on the chest.*

Scarf

1 Position the Scarf template on the fold of doubled fabric, as shown on the template, and cut out the piece.

2 With right sides together, fold the scarf in half lengthwise. Using a ¼″ seam allowance, sew across an end of the scarf and down the length, stopping in the middle. Sew across the other end of the scarf and down the length, stopping about 1″ before you meet the opposite stitches. (Refer to the illustration for Belt, Step 2, page 57, for guidance.)

3 Turn right side out, using turning tubes, through the hole left in the center of the scarf. Press.

4 Make 6 tassels from embroidery floss. For each tassel, cut 3 lengths of floss, 3″ each. Embroidery floss has 6 strands, but don't separate them.

5 Cut 2 lengths of floss, 7″ each. Pull apart the strands, 2 at a time. This will give you 6 lengths of floss (2 strands each) for tying the 6 tassels.

6 Fold a 3″ bundle of floss over the smallest turning tube. If you don't have turning tubes, you can use a 2.75mm knitting needle or crochet hook. Wrap a 7″ length of floss (2 strands) around the tassel, leaving a tail hanging as you begin to wrap. Wrap several times and knot the 2 ends. Repeat to make a total of 6 tassels.

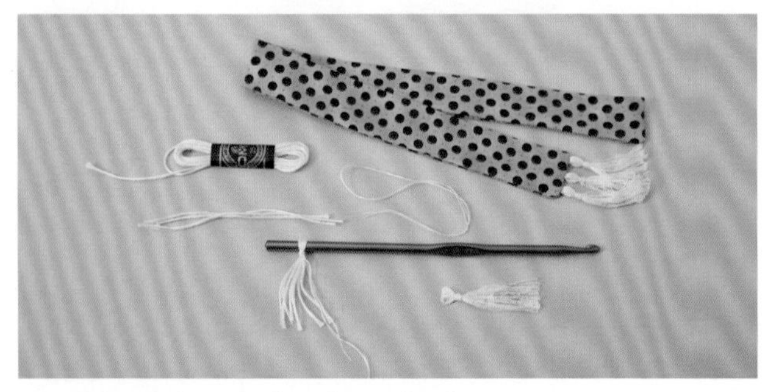

Assemble tassels to stitch to the scarf ends.

7 Sew 3 tassels to each end of the scarf.

Tip *If you knit or crochet, you can quickly work up a scarf from crochet cotton or lightweight yarn. A knit or crocheted scarf should measure about 1″ × 16″ before the fringe is added.*

Making the Shoes

The shoes are sewn by hand using a whipstitch (or a blanket stitch, if you prefer). If you match the thread to the shoe color, the stitching will not stand out. If you *want* the stitching to stand out, sew with a contrasting thread color.

1 On the wrong side of the shoe vinyl, trace the Shoe template 2 times, then flip the template over and trace again 2 times (for right and left shoes). Trace the Shoe Sole template 2 times, and trace the Shoe Toe template 2 times. Mark the sole at the center of the heel, as shown on the template pattern.

2 Cut out the shoes, soles, and toes on the traced lines.

3 With wrong sides together, sew the center front shoe seam from the toe to the top edge. Then sew the back of the shoe from the heel to the top edge.

4 Sew the sole to the bottom edge of the shoe. Line up the mark you made on the heel of the sole with the seam at the back of the shoe. Sew from the heel around the side of the shoe, stopping where the sole starts to taper in, as indicated on the template pattern. Sew the other side, starting again from the heel.

5 Join the toe to the shoe along each side, starting at the point. The base of the toe should overlap the sole slightly. Sew the overlap in place with a few stitches.

6 Use the Shoe Trim template to cut 2 pieces of fur.

7 Wrap the fur around the top of the shoe with the right side facing out and the ends meeting at the seam at the back of the shoe. Using matching thread so the stitches won't show, whipstitch the fur to the top edge of the shoe. Stitch the ends of the fur together where they meet at the back of the shoe.

Assembling the shoe

8 Sew a ½″ jingle bell to the point of each shoe. Push a bit of stuffing into the tip of the shoe where the foot won't reach. Fit the shoes onto the doll, putting the foot in and then using a dowel to push the heel down into the shoe.

Making the Head

Refer to Making the Doll's Head (page 9), Sculpting the Face (page 10), Coloring the Face (page 14), and Adding Eyelids and Lashes (page 17).

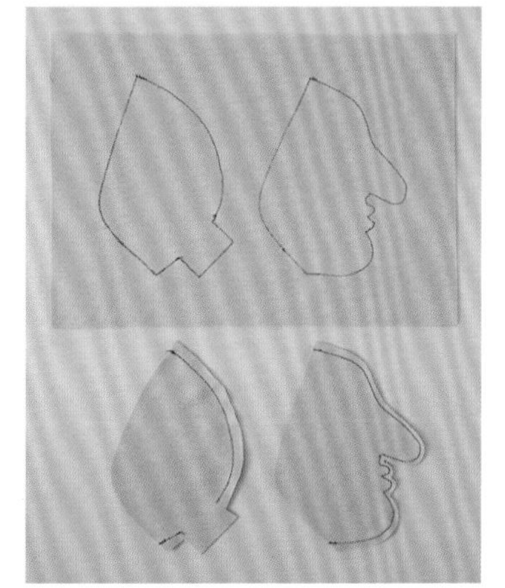

Trace, sew, and cut out the head pieces.

Felting Wool Eyebrows

Use a #40 felting needle to attach wool eyebrows. It takes only a small bit of wool to make the eyebrows. You can use wool roving or 100% wool yarn. It can be the same wool you use for the hair or a slightly darker color.

NOTE

A felting needle in size #40 or #42 is a fine needle. As the numbers get lower, the needles are larger and more coarse. The Pincushion Girls project (page 38) includes instructions for working with wool and felting needles and offers important information that can be used for this project also.

Wool is laid on the head and the felting needle is poked through into the stuffing of the head. The wool gets tangled with the stuffing in the head and becomes attached without the aid of glue or sewing. When you use a felting needle to attach one wool piece to another, you can poke away as much as you want. However, when using the felting needle to attach wool to fabric (as in this project), continued poking in one spot will create a hole in the fabric. Be mindful of this as you attach wool to the doll's head. It doesn't take much poking to attach the wool. A gentle tug will let you know if it's attached.

1 Cut a few pieces of wool (roving or yarn) about 1″ long.

2 Lay the center of the 1″ wool across the brow line. Spread the fibers out over the desired length of the eyebrow (about 1″ to 1¼″).

3 Using a quick up-and-down motion, poke the needle into the head ¼″ to ½″ deep. Poke along the brow line in the center of the fibers.

4 Stand the wool up from the head with your fingers. Poke a few times along the outer edge of the fibers and the brows will stay standing up.

5 Trim the eyebrows to ¼″.

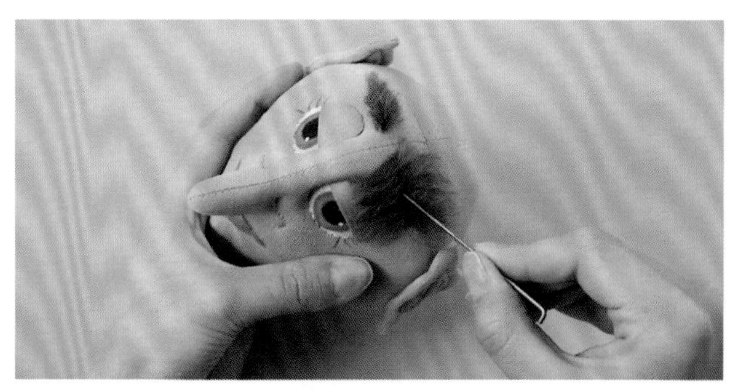

It doesn't take much poking with a felting needle to attach the eyebrows.

Making the Ears

1. Trace the Ear template 2 times on doubled fabric—the same fabric used to make the head.

2. Sew on the traced line, using a very short stitch length.

3. Cut out each ear, leaving a ⅛″ seam allowance.

4. Lay the ears on a work surface so you have a right and a left ear facing you. Cut a slit on the back of each ear, being careful to cut through only a single thickness of fabric.

5. Use tiny turning tubes to turn each ear right side out through the cut you made in the back.

6. Stuff the ears softly. Push a small scrap of fabric into the hole to cover the stuffing.

7. Use a water-soluble fabric marker to draw the line detail for the inside of the ear. (Refer to the Ear template, or create your own details.) Sew on the drawn lines, either by hand or using an open-toe or clear presser foot on your sewing machine.

8. Wet the entire ear with a paintbrush. Use the same colors to shade the ear that you used for the face, rubbing on color with the side of the pencil and blending it with a paintbrush.

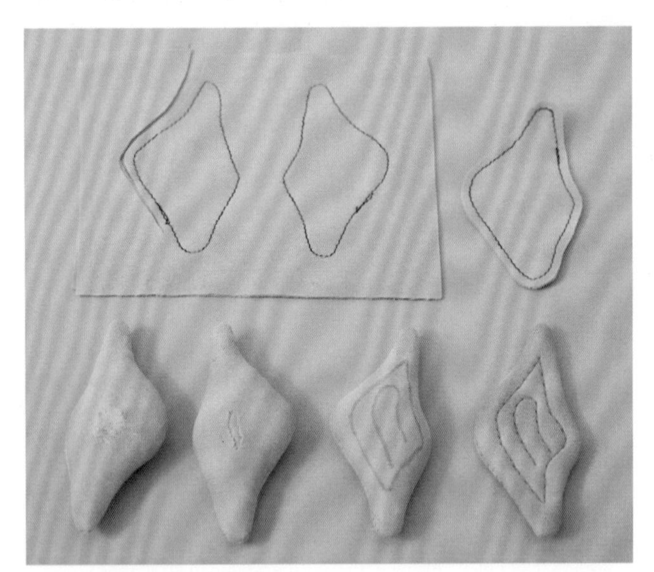

Step-by-step ear assembly

9. Pin the ears evenly to the head, positioning them over the head side seams. Stitch to the head at the center of the back of each ear, leaving the earlobe and the top of the ear unattached.

The earlobe and top of the ear are not stitched down.

Attaching the Head

Push your finger up into the stuffing in the head to make a space for inserting the neck. Push the neck up into the head. Ladder stitch the head securely to the neck.

Adding the Hat and Hair

Making the Hat

1. Trace the Hat template on the wrong side of doubled fabric.

2. Sew directly on the traced line, leaving the hat open at the bottom, as shown on the template.

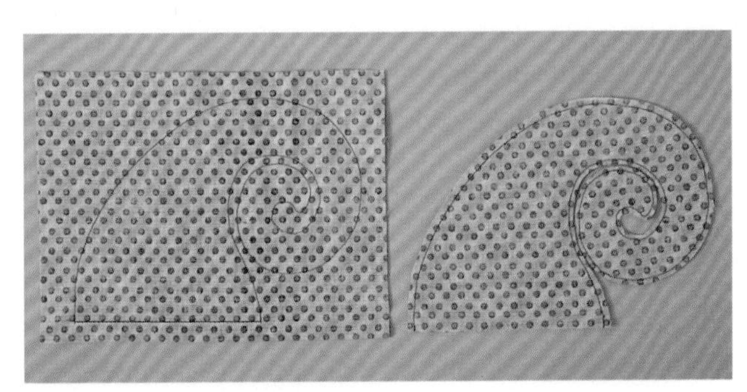

Trace, stitch, and cut out the hat.

3. Cut out the hat, leaving a ¼″ seam allowance. Cut carefully between the sewing lines on the corkscrew at the top of the hat. At the bottom, cut directly on the line that you didn't sew. Turn the hat right side out.

4. Trace the Hat Band template (on the fold) and cut out.

5. With right sides together, sew a ¼″ seam to join the ends of the band.

6. Slide the band over the hat, right sides together. Pin so the corkscrew top of the hat is in front and the seam of the band is at the center back of the hat. Sew the hat to the band.

7. Turn the raw edge of the band under ½″ and press.

8. Stuff the entire hat. It's a little tricky getting started and working around the corkscrew shape, so take your time. Sew a jingle bell to the end of the hat.

Creating the Hairstyle

1. Position the hat on the doll's head and pin in place. Use a purple disappearing fabric marker to mark where the hat sits on the head, and then remove the hat. The part of the head that will be covered by the hat won't need hair. The hair will be attached just inside the marks you've made.

2. Cut several pieces of wool roving, each 5″ long.

3. Lay a piece of wool roving on the head so that the center of the length of wool is inside the marking for the hat. Needle felt the wool to the head at the center of the piece. Then fold the wool piece in half so both ends point toward the neck, and needle felt on the fold. Fill in with wool hair from ear to ear around the back of the head.

4. Lay a 5″ length of wool in front of the ear, making sure the center of the wool piece is inside the hat line. Needle felt to the head at the center. Then fold over the upper portion of wool toward the face, and needle felt on the fold. Repeat on the other side of the head.

5. Give the doll a haircut to even up the ends of the wool pieces.

Attaching the Hat

1. Place the hat on the head. Make sure all the folds of wool are tucked up under the hat. Pin the hat in place.

2. Ladder stitch the hat to the head. Stitch in the crease of the hem you pressed earlier in the hat band, stitching through the hair and into the fabric of the head.

Stitch the hat to the head through the hair.

Finishing Touches

Decide what job your elf has at the North Pole. Be creative as you search for props or make your own. Consider the person you are making the elf for as you make these choices.

The sample doll has a wooden truck found at the craft store. The paintbrush in his other hand is made from a wooden chopstick—the kind that comes as an attached pair. You can whittle the soft wood as if you're sharpening a pencil with a knife, or you can sand it with 120-grit sandpaper.

1. Break the chopsticks apart. Mark the area to be carved (or sanded) on the fat end of the chopstick.

2. With a knife, score lines for the paintbrush's silver band. Shave just enough of the wood to create an edge for the band. If you are using the sandpaper method, you can simply paint on the silver band.

3. Carve a small V in the center of the end of the "bristles." To achieve the dip without carving, wrap 120-grit sandpaper over the edge of a table or counter and sand away the center of the paintbrush bristles.

4. Carve or sand the corner to round the end of the bristles.

5. Paint the chopstick with acrylic paints. Paint the bristles black or brown and then dip the very tip into a bright color to represent paint.

6. Drill a tiny hole through the chopstick. Sew the paintbrush to the doll's hand through the hole.

The soft wood of the chopstick is easily shaped with a knife or sandpaper.

Wrapping the Present

The Christmas package on which Lyle sits is a cardboard box covered with fabric. Wrap it with fabric the same way you'd wrap a gift with paper, using white craft glue to attach the fabric to the box.

Making the Fabric Bow

1. Cut 1 shape using the Present Bow Tie template.

2. Trace the Present Bow template (on the fold) on the wrong side of doubled fabric. Sew on the traced line, leaving open both ends as shown on the template. Trim the stitching, leaving a ¼″ seam allowance.

3. Turn the bow right side out. Press.

4. Fold under the ends of the bow, overlapping them in the center. Make a few stitches in the center through all the layers to hold the bow together.

5. Fold under both sides of the bow tie, as shown on the template, and press. Wrap the tie around the middle of the bow. Overlap the ends on the bottom so the seam will be hidden when the bow is attached to the package. Stitch the tie to secure the center of the bow.

6. Cut a 1″-wide strip of bow fabric to wrap around the box. Glue in place. Glue on the bow at an end of the package.

Forming the bow

Storing the Elf

Store your elves with as much care as you'd take for your other treasured holiday decorations. Make a keepsake box for your creations, choosing a box with a lift-off lid instead of flaps. See Storing the Tooth Fairy (page 35) for more information. If you make an elf for a child, he or she could have a part in making the box. Copy photos on plain paper and decoupage them onto the box. Add Christmas memories over the years, and over time your box will become a collage that's as important as its contents.

Gallery of Elves

Jingle

Jingle's reading glasses are 3″ wide. In lieu of buttons, ¼″ jingle bells are stitched to his shirt. The bands around his shoes were constructed in the same way as the glove bands. A black-and-white checked fabric cut on the diagonal creates a bold pattern on the belt. The computer-printed sled directions are secured to his hand with a tiny stitch. Notice that none of the fabrics have a Christmas theme, yet the red, black, and white prints feel quite festive.

Jingle was recently promoted to the sled department and has some concerns about his sled-building abilities. The sleds seem to be going together easily enough, but he doesn't know what to do with all the leftover parts. The directions don't say anything about leftover parts!

Jaxson

Jaxson has wool eyebrows attached with a felting needle. Synthetic curls are stitched to his head under the hat. Snowflake buttons on his gloves and shoes enhance the snowflake print fabric of his hat and gloves. The bow template was enlarged to adorn his big package.

Jaxson is in charge of holiday decorations. Replacing burned-out bulbs is a full-time job at the North Pole. It's also one of the most stressful positions—we all know how easily those strings of lights get tangled!

Elden

Elden is the head candy maker and prefers to be called the Sugar Chef. He has short, stumpy legs and a round belly, the result of taste-testing his creations. His jacket is made using the shirt pattern. Fabric stiffener was applied to the sack so it could hold his candy. Elden's wool hair and eyebrows were attached with a felting needle.

Tiny Flower Fairy

5″ sitting doll

Neenah

This delicate little fairy with a sweetly simple face sits just 5″ tall above her flower. Her body is made from a batik fabric that becomes her outfit. She can be embellished with tiny rose-buds, ribbon, and beads. The templates for this project offer three different leg positions, giving you the choice of a standing, sitting, or flying fairy. There are also templates for three wing shapes, or you could create your own shape.

The fairies are enhanced with folded fabric flowers made using techniques from origami (Japanese paper folding) and *kanzashi* (ornaments for traditional Japanese hair styles). Origami begins with a square that is folded into a sculptural shape. *Hana* (flower) *kanzashi* uses a technique called *tsumami* (pinching) to create delicate blossoms from squares of silk. Using both methods, the flowers for this pattern are folded from squares of cotton fabric.

Please read through the chapter before you begin. The tiny fairy comes together quickly using the trace-sew-cut technique. Turning tubes are highly recommended for turning the very small body parts. Because of the size of this project, small-scale prints work best. Take a look at the template sizes before you choose fabric.

Materials

See page 8 for lists of general sewing and doll-making equipment.

Fabric for fairy:

- 6″ × 8″ flesh-tone cotton fabric for head and hands (Use a quilter's-quality fabric with a high thread count.)
- ¼ yard (or 1 fat quarter) batik fabric for body, arms, and legs
- 4″ × 6″ cotton fabric for shoes (You can use the wing fabric, choose a fabric to complement the body fabric, or make the leg and shoe from the body fabric in a single piece.)
- 10″ × 10″ cotton print fabric for wings

Fabric for flowers and leaves:

- 6″ × 12″ cotton print fabric to make 10 petals for 2″ flower
- 8″ × 14″ cotton print fabric to make 8 petals for 3″ flower
- 18″ × 18″ cotton print fabric to make 16 petals for 4″ flower
- 12″ × 16″ green cotton print fabric for leaves
- 2″ × 2″ fabric scrap for flower center

Other supplies:

- ¾ yard of ⅛″-wide ribbon for wrists, ankles, and neck (*optional*)
- 2 stamens for fairy antennae (available in the floral, bridal, or cake-decorating section of the craft store)
- Glitter glue for eyes and stamens
- Polyester fiberfill
- 5 white pipe cleaners for wings and leaves
- Artist-quality watercolor pencils for shading face
- Quilter's Vinyl (by C&T Publishing, *optional*)

Templates Required

You'll use the following templates (pages 93 and 94) for the Neenah Tiny Flower Fairy:

> Head, Body, Arm A, Arm B, Leg B, Wing A, Small Leaf, Medium Leaf, Large Leaf, Large Flower Center. The Tiny Fairies in the Gallery (pages 76 and 77) use the alternate templates provided: Leg A, Leg C, Wing B, Wing C, and Small Flower Center.

All templates are traced onto 2 layers of fabric placed right sides together, unless otherwise indicated.

NOTE

I used Quilter's Vinyl (see Resources, page 95) to make templates for the body, arms, legs, and wings. The see-through vinyl makes it easy to position a template on specific areas of the fabric design, allowing you to place the print exactly where you want it on this tiny body. It takes more fabric to lay out the templates this way, but the end result is worth it.

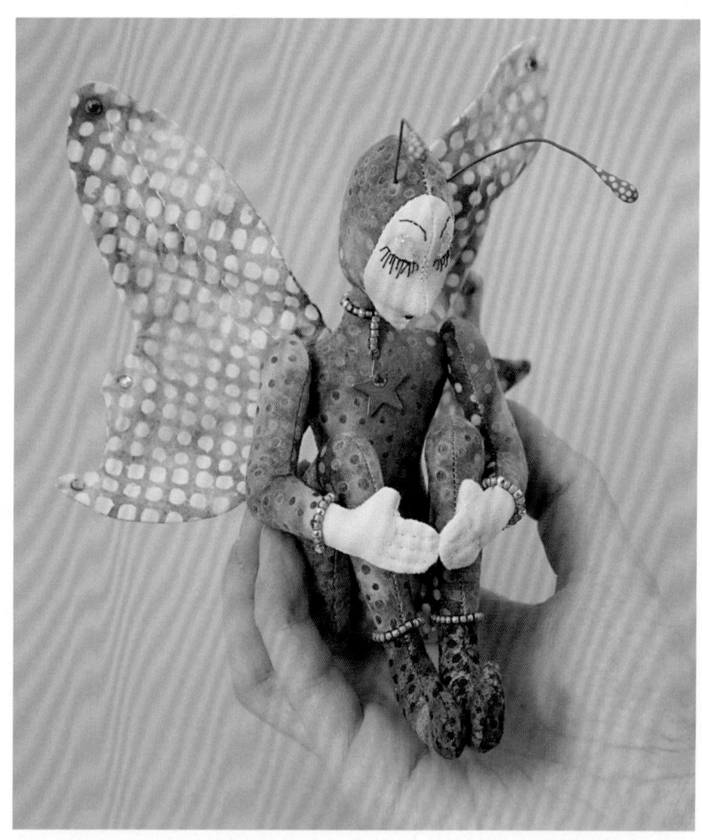

Small-scale prints work well with dainty fairies, such as this sitting fairy (page 77).

Constructing the Body

Use a very short machine stitch length when sewing the body parts. The trace-sew-cut technique is used for all the body parts. All pieces are cut leaving a ⅛″ seam allowance. When working with such a small seam allowance, you don't need to clip the curves.

1. Trace the Body template with a mechanical pencil on the wrong side of doubled fabric.

2. Sew the body with matching thread. Leave the neck open for turning and stuffing, as shown on the template.

3. Cut out the sewn body, leaving a ⅛″ seam allowance. At the neck opening, cut directly on the traced line.

4. Turn the body right side out, using turning tubes. Stuff with fiberfill through the neck opening. Turn under the raw edge of the neck.

Tip *I find turning tubes helpful as a stuffing tool when I'm working on small body parts with tiny stuffing holes.*

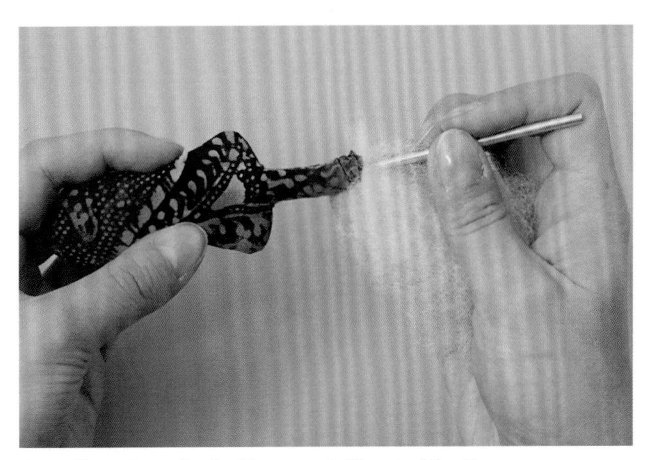

A small turning tube doubles as a stuffing tool for these tiny body parts.

Making the Arms

1. Cut 4 squares of fabric 3″ × 3″ for the arms.

2. Cut 4 rectangles 2″ × 3″ from the hand fabric.

3. Sew an arm square to a hand rectangle along the 3″ edge. Trim the seam allowance to ⅛″. Repeat to make 4 arm-hand pieces.

4. Press the seam allowances toward the hand fabric. This step is important, because later on when you are stuffing this tiny arm, the seam allowance will lie in the direction the stuffing is being pushed into the arm, letting you push it through the tiny wrist area without resistance.

The arm fabric is sewn to the hand fabric, and then the arm and hand are traced as a single piece.

5. With right sides together, line up the seams on 2 arm-hand pieces. Trace the Arm template onto the fabric, lining up the wrist line on the template with the seam where the 2 fabrics are joined. Repeat the process for the second arm.

6. Sew on the traced line, leaving the stuffing hole open as shown on the template. Repeat for the second arm.

7. Cut out the arms with a ⅛″ seam allowance. Cut the tab at the stuffing hole directly on the traced line.

8. Use turning tubes to turn the arms right side out.

9. Put a very small amount of fiberfill stuffing into the hand. Use your sewing machine or hand sew the separation lines between the fingers, as shown on the template.

10. Stuff the rest of the arm. Close the stuffing hole using a ladder stitch.

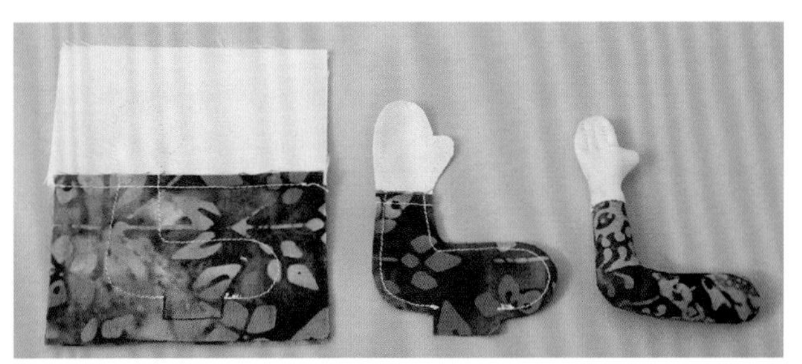

Making the arms

Making the Legs

There are 3 templates for the legs. Leg A is straight, Leg B is slightly bent, and Leg C is fully bent, allowing you to make your fairy standing, sitting, or flying. For a standing fairy, use templates A and B. For a flying fairy, use templates B and C. For a sitting fairy, use either templates B and C or templates A and B.

To make the shoes a different color than the legs, prepare the fabric the same way as for the arms and hands. If you choose to make the entire leg with the body fabric, skip Steps 1–3 and begin by tracing the leg template on the wrong side of doubled fabric (Step 4).

Leg positions A, B, and C

1. *To make a straight leg (A),* cut 2 rectangles 2″ × 5″ from the body fabric. For the shoes, cut 2 rectangles 2″ × 3″ from shoe fabric.

   To make a bent leg (B or C), cut 2 rectangles 3″ × 4″ from the body fabric. For the shoes, cut 2 rectangles 2″ × 3″ from the shoe fabric.

2. Sew a leg piece to each shoe piece as shown in the photo (below). Trim the seam allowance to ⅛″. Notice that the shoe fabric on the bent legs is offset to a side of the leg fabric, and that the shoe fabric for the straight leg is wider than the leg fabric. The shape of the shoe requires the fabric to be offset as shown.

Join the leg and shoe fabrics as shown for leg A, B, or C. White thread was used here for clarity, but you should match your thread to the fabric.

3. Press the seam so the seam allowance lies on the shoe fabric. This step is important, because later on when you are stuffing this tiny leg, the seam allowance will lie in the direction the stuffing is being pushed into the leg. This will let you push the stuffing through the tiny ankle without resistance.

4. With right sides together, line up the seam on 2 leg-shoe units and pin together. Trace the leg template onto the fabric, lining up the ankle line on the template with the seam where the fabrics are joined. Repeat for the second leg.

5. Sew on the traced line, leaving the stuffing hole open as shown on the template. Repeat for the second leg.

6. Cut out the legs, leaving a ⅛″ seam allowance. Cut the tab at the stuffing hole directly on the traced line.

7. Use turning tubes to turn the legs right side out.

8. Stuff the legs firmly with fiberfill. Close the stuffing hole using a ladder stitch.

Making the Head

1. Cut 2 rectangles 1½″ × 3″ from the flesh-tone fabric and 2 rectangles 2″ × 3″ from the body fabric.

2. Sew a flesh-tone rectangle to a body-color rectangle along a 3″ side. Repeat with the remaining 2 rectangles.

3. Press the seam allowance toward the body fabric so no shadow will show through the flesh-tone fabric. With right sides together, line up the seams and pin together.

4. Trace the Head template onto the fabric. Refer to the template pattern for placement of the seam on the head.

5. Sew on the traced line, leaving the neck open as shown on the template.

6. Cut out the head, leaving a ⅛″ seam allowance.

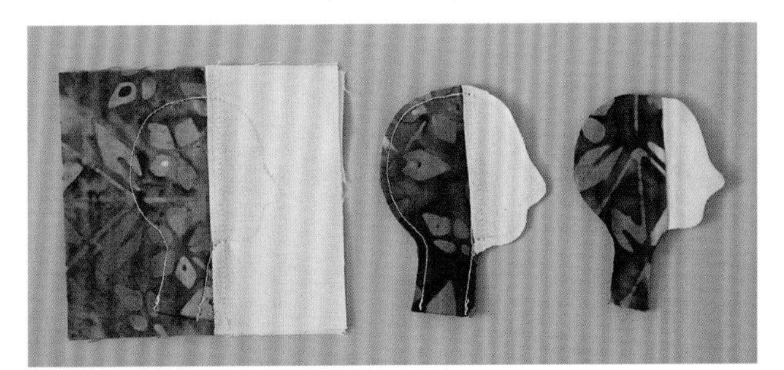

Prepare the head fabrics the same way you did the arm and leg fabrics.

7. Use turning tubes to turn the head right side out. Stuff the head with fiberfill and fold under the raw edge of the neck.

Creating the Face

1. Use a single strand of black thread to stitch the eyes and eyebrows. You can stitch freehand or draw the eyes and brows with a disappearing fabric marker. Knot the thread, insert the needle through the opening in the neck, and come out at the eyelashes.

2. Make tiny stitches for the line of the closed eyelid. Stitch lashes in different lengths. Stitch the eyebrows. When you are finished, knot the thread on the inside of the neck.

3. Use 2 strands of red or pink thread to make a tiny stitch for the mouth—or you can choose not to give the doll a mouth at all. Knot the thread on the inside of the neck.

4. Wet the head with clean water and a paintbrush. Use the side of a pink watercolor pencil to rub color onto the cheeks. Blend the color into the cheeks with the paintbrush. Add a hint of color to the eyelid area with a light brown pencil.

5. Let the head dry, or speed up the process by using a hair dryer.

6. Use a toothpick to add a bit of glitter glue to the eyelids for some sparkle.

Add facial features and color.

Assembling the Body

1. Pin the legs to the body, making adjustments until you are happy with their position. Stitch the legs neatly to the body with matching thread so the stitches will be hidden.

2. Pin the arms to the body. As you position the arms, consider whether or not the fairy will be holding a flower. Stitch the arms neatly to the body with matching thread so the stitches won't show.

3. Stitch the neck of the head to the neck of the body, folding the raw edges under. Some fabrics fray more than others when you work with them, so the template patterns provide ample fabric in the neck area to allow for possible fraying. Make sure each piece is stuffed to the top so there won't be a hollow area in the neck.

Dressing the Doll

Using a print fabric for the body of the fairy makes her look like she's already dressed. How much you embellish her is up to you. You can cover the seams at her neck, wrists, and ankles with seed beads sewn right onto the body, or you can simply tie ribbon around the seams.

If you enjoy working with beads, you could sew beads or sequins to the fairy's entire body. If you want to do this, choose fabric with a print that offers beading options. You could also attach strings of beads to create a skirt, or make a skirt from ribbons with tiny rosebuds sewn to the ends.

Attaching Antennae

Adding antennae to the head makes this fairy look like a delicate little butterfly. I used flower stamens to create the look of antennae. These can be found at the craft store in the floral, bridal accessories, or cake-decorating section. You'll get a bundle of them in a package, usually white. Choose the shape you like.

1. Paint the stamens with acrylic paint in whatever color you wish. Add glitter glue to the ends for sparkle. Allow to dry.

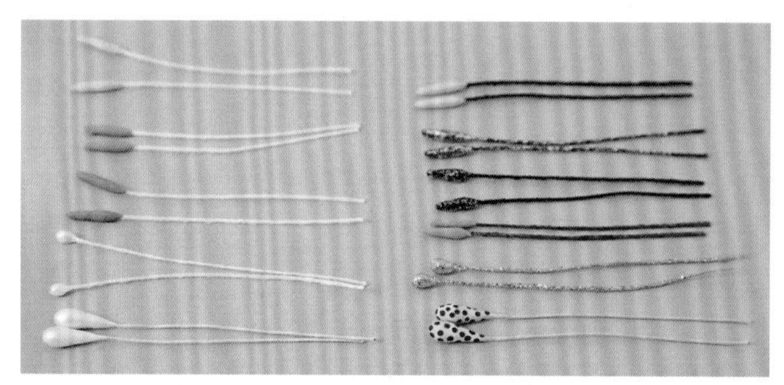

The stamens at left are as purchased. Those at right have been customized with acrylic paint and glitter.

2. Stick a very thick needle into the head where you want to place an antenna. Wiggle it to create a hole.

3. Dip the end of the stamen into white craft glue and then stick it into the hole you've made in the head. Repeat for the other antenna.

Making the Wings

Just as you deliberately positioned the fabric design on the body, you can fussy cut the wings the same way. It requires more fabric to lay out the templates this way, so keep that in mind as you search for the perfect fabric. The distance between the repeats in the print will help you determine how much fabric you need. Also be aware that if the design goes only in one direction, you won't be able to create the mirror image you need for right and left wings.

I used batik fabrics on the sample dolls in this chapter. One thing you may notice about many batiks is that the wrong side of the fabric often looks as good as the right side. It can be hard to tell which is which. This makes batiks a great choice for mirror-image wings.

Tip *If you are making matching (mirror-image) wings, use Quilter's Vinyl to make the wing template. The see-through vinyl will allow you to easily place the template exactly where you want it on the design in the fabric.*

1. Cut 4 squares 5″ × 5″ for the wings. Fold under an edge of each square ¼″ and press.

2. Place 2 squares right sides together, aligning the folded edges. Lay the template on the fabric so the folded fabric edge is lined up with the center of the wing. (The center of the wing is marked "open" on the template pattern.) Trace the Wing template (A, B, or C) on the wrong side of the doubled fabric.

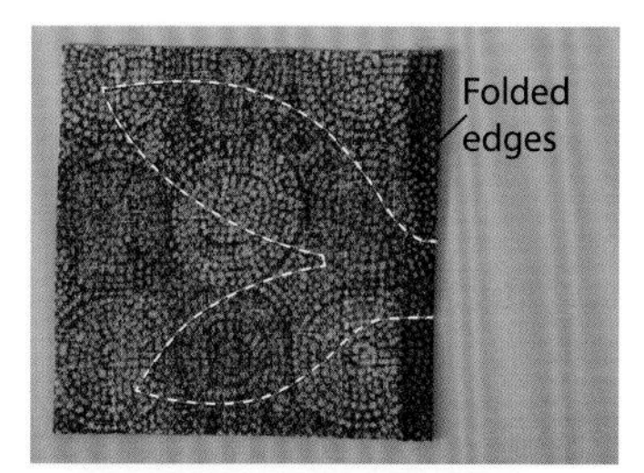

Folding the fabric edge before sewing the wing creates a neat opening for inserting pipe cleaners and sewing to the opposite wing.

3. Sew around the wing on the traced line, leaving the center open where the fabric is folded.

4. Cut out the wing, leaving a ⅛″ seam allowance. Turn right side out and press.

5. Use a purple disappearing fabric marker to draw a ¼″-wide channel for the pipe cleaner as shown on the template pattern (page 93). Choose a matching thread color if you want the stitches to blend into the fabric, a contrasting thread color if you want the stitches to stand out. Sew the channel on each wing.

Sew a channel on the wing to insert a pipe cleaner.

6. Bend under an end of a pipe cleaner so it won't poke through the fabric. Push the bent end all the way into the channel. Cut off the excess pipe cleaner sticking out of the wing. If your wing has 2 channels like Wing A, bend under each end of the pipe cleaner and push one end into each channel.

7. Repeat Steps 2–6 for the second wing.

8. Butt the wings together at the center and sew them together.

9. Sew the wings to the fairy's back. Bend the pipe cleaners to give the wings shape.

Sew the wings to the back of the body.

Making the Fabric Flower

The project doll sits on a stack of three flowers that are glued together at the center. The base flower has sixteen petals made from 4″ × 4″ squares, the center flower has eight petals made from 3″ × 3″ squares, and the top flower has ten petals made from 2″ × 2″ squares.

You can make the fabric flowers any size you choose. Each petal is folded from a square of fabric, and the finished flower will be approximately the size of that square. If the petals are made from 4″ × 4″ squares, for example, you can expect the finished flower to measure about 4″ across. The larger the square, the easier it will be to fold. For this reason, I recommend that your first flower be made with 4″ × 4″ squares as you learn the folding sequence.

Press the fabric and lay it out wrong side up. Use a ruler and a pencil to mark the size of squares you want. Cut out the squares; if you have quilting tools, you can use a rotary cutter and quilting rulers for this.

Thread a needle with doubled thread in a matching color. As each petal is finished, you will string it onto the thread.

1. Fold the square in half to make a triangle. Lay the triangle on a table with the fold at the top.

2. Take the points of the triangle on the left and right, and fold them down to the point at the bottom. The folded edges will meet at the center, forming a square.

3. Turn the square over, keeping the top point at the top.

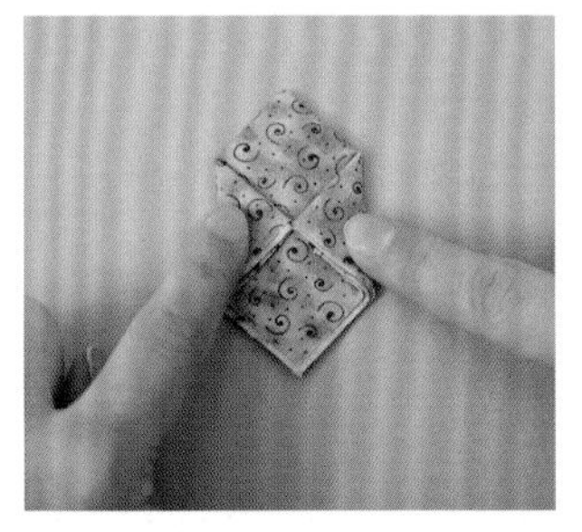

4. Fold over the left and right points so they meet in the center of the square.

5. Fold the right side over onto the left side. Don't let go, or the fabric will pop open.

6. Pick up the petal so the folded end is on the left and the raw pointed edges are on the right. Square off the raw edges of the fabric, cutting through all layers.

7. String the petal onto the threaded needle you prepared earlier, inserting the needle in the center of the petal about ⅛″ from the cut edge.

8. Repeat Steps 1–7 until you have the number of petals you need. Pull the thread and tie it in a knot to create the flower; don't pull so tightly that the petals can't lie evenly. Both sides of the petal look nice, so either side may be used as the top.

Tip *Of course, your artistic license lets you make changes wherever you want in your flowers. I made all the flowers in the photo below using the folding technique described above. Experiment with different petal sizes, combine fabrics, add layers, or use more than one petal size in a single flower. Open the ends of the petals to make them wide, or iron the petals flat. Turn the petal over and use the other side. Showcase part of the fabric print as the flower center, or use a vintage button. The folded flowers will also make great embellishments for other craft projects.*

Flower Center

For the middle of the flower, you can glue on a button or make a fabric "button." Gluing the fabric center to the flower will hold the petals in place. To give the flower more stability or to give the underside a more finished look, glue a small circle of fabric to the bottom as well.

1. Trace the Flower Center template on the wrong side of a scrap of fabric.
2. Sew a running stitch around the circle on the traced line.
3. Cut out the circle ⅛″ from the stitches.
4. Place stuffing in the circle, pull the thread ends to gather the fabric around the stuffing, and knot the thread.
5. Glue the flower center, gathered side down, to the center of the flower.

Sewing a running stitch before you cut out the circle helps keep the edge from fraying.

Leaves

The leaves are made the same way as the fairy's wings. The sample doll was made with a large, a small, and two medium leaves. Add as many leaves as you like to your blooms.

1. Cut 2 fabric rectangles for each leaf. Be sure the rectangles are at least 1″ wider and 1″ longer than the desired finished leaf. Fold under a short edge of the fabric ¼″. Repeat with a second fabric rectangle. Place rectangles right sides together, aligning the folded edges. Lay the Leaf template on the wrong side of doubled fabric so the folded edges are lined up with the straight end of the leaf. Trace the template.
2. Sew around the leaf on the traced line, leaving the straight end open at the folded edges.
3. Cut out the leaf, leaving a ⅛″ seam allowance. Turn right side out and press.
4. The pipe cleaners are added to the leaves the same way as they were to the wings. Use a purple disappearing fabric marker to draw a ¼″-wide channel for the pipe cleaner as shown on the template. Choose matching thread if you want the stitches to blend into the fabric, contrasting thread if you want them to stand out. Sew the channel on the leaf.

Construct the leaves the same way you made the wings.

5. Bend under an end of a pipe cleaner. Push the pipe cleaner, bent end first, all the way to the end of the channel. Cut off the excess pipe cleaner that sticks out of the leaf.

6. Sew or glue the leaf to the underside of the flower.

Attaching the Fairy to the Flower

1. Position the fairy on the flower center and use pins to hold her in place.
2. Sew her bottom and legs to the flower center.
3. Bend up the large leaf and sew her hand to the edge of the leaf.

Sewing the fairy to both the flower center and the leaf will hold her securely in position.

Gallery of Fairies

The blue-winged fairy sits atop a two-layer flower, its bottom layer composed of eight petals folded from 4″ × 4″ squares, its second layer of eight petals folded from 3″ × 3″ squares. The small flower is glued to the large flower. The flower center (made from the Large Flower Center template) is glued to the middle of the small flower. The base of the doll's body is stitched to the flower center. Two large leaves, glued to the bottom of the flower, curl up around the fairy, and her hands are stitched to them. One leg was made from the Leg B template, the other from the Leg C template.

Leg templates A and B were used to create this lounging fairy, whose wings were cut from a batik fabric with a larger-scale print than the body fabric. The shape of the wings follows the print in the fabric to make mirror image wings. Seed beads strung with silver flower beads adorn the fairy's wrists, ankles, and neck. Stamens were painted with purple acrylic paint and glitter glue was brushed on the ends.

This purple fairy's legs, made from Leg B and C templates, are in position for flying. The 2″ flower she holds has ten petals and a glued-on center made from a pink bead sewn to a purple button. Pink seed beads encircle the doll's face, neck, wrists, and ankles. A jump ring is attached to her back for hanging her with clear thread.

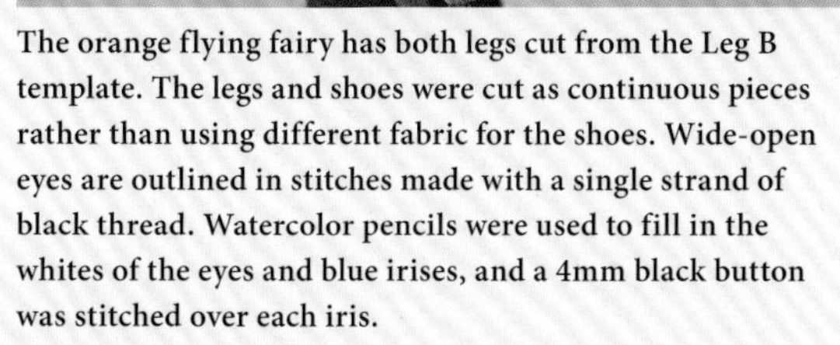

The orange flying fairy has both legs cut from the Leg B template. The legs and shoes were cut as continuous pieces rather than using different fabric for the shoes. Wide-open eyes are outlined in stitches made with a single strand of black thread. Watercolor pencils were used to fill in the whites of the eyes and blue irises, and a 4mm black button was stitched over each iris.

The Leg C template was used to create this sitting fairy, whose hands are stitched together at the fingertips to hold her arms in place. A star charm is attached to the seed beads that encircle her neck, and tiny rhinestones are glued to her wings. A toothpick dipped in pink paint was used to apply dots to her blue antennae.

Template Patterns

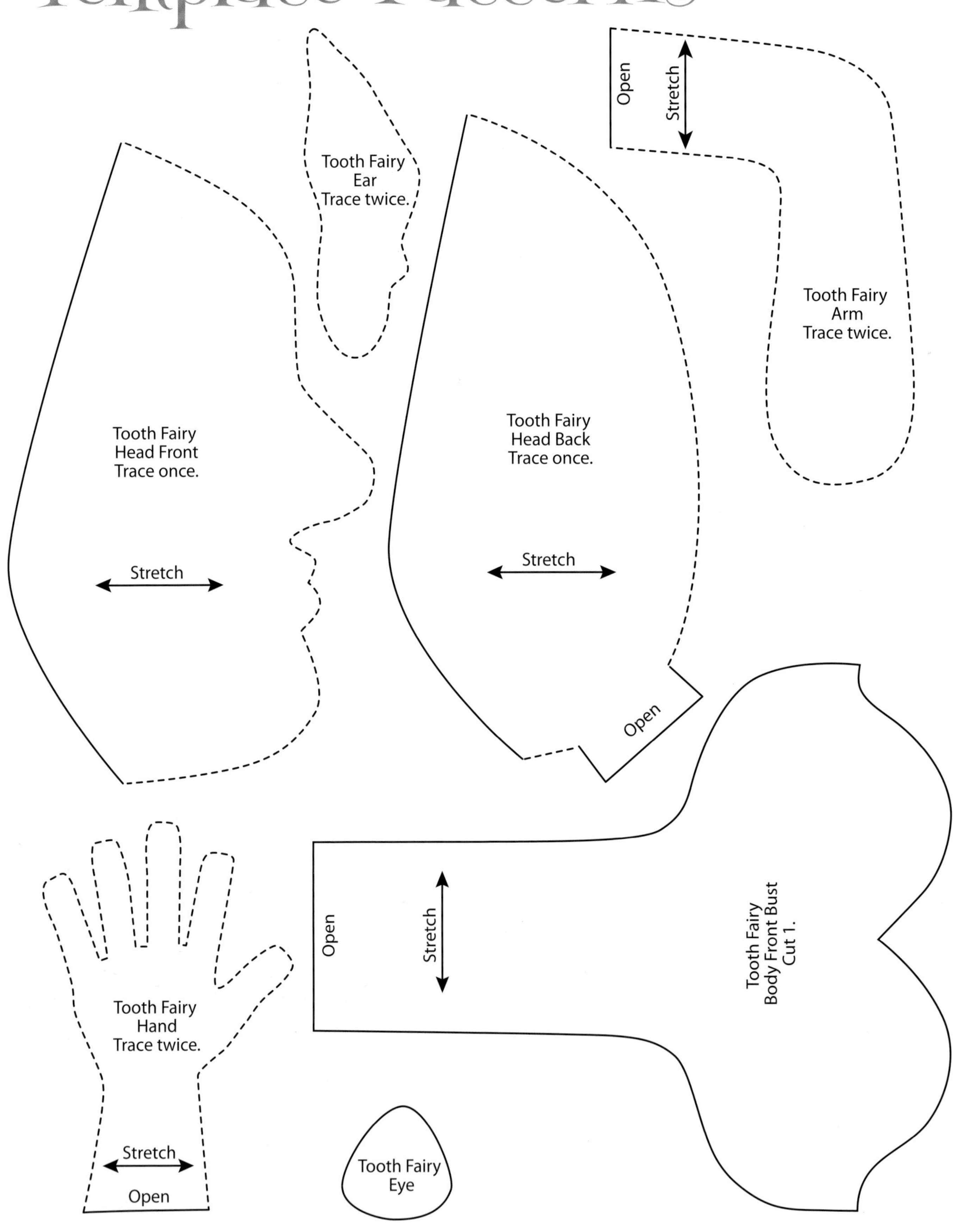

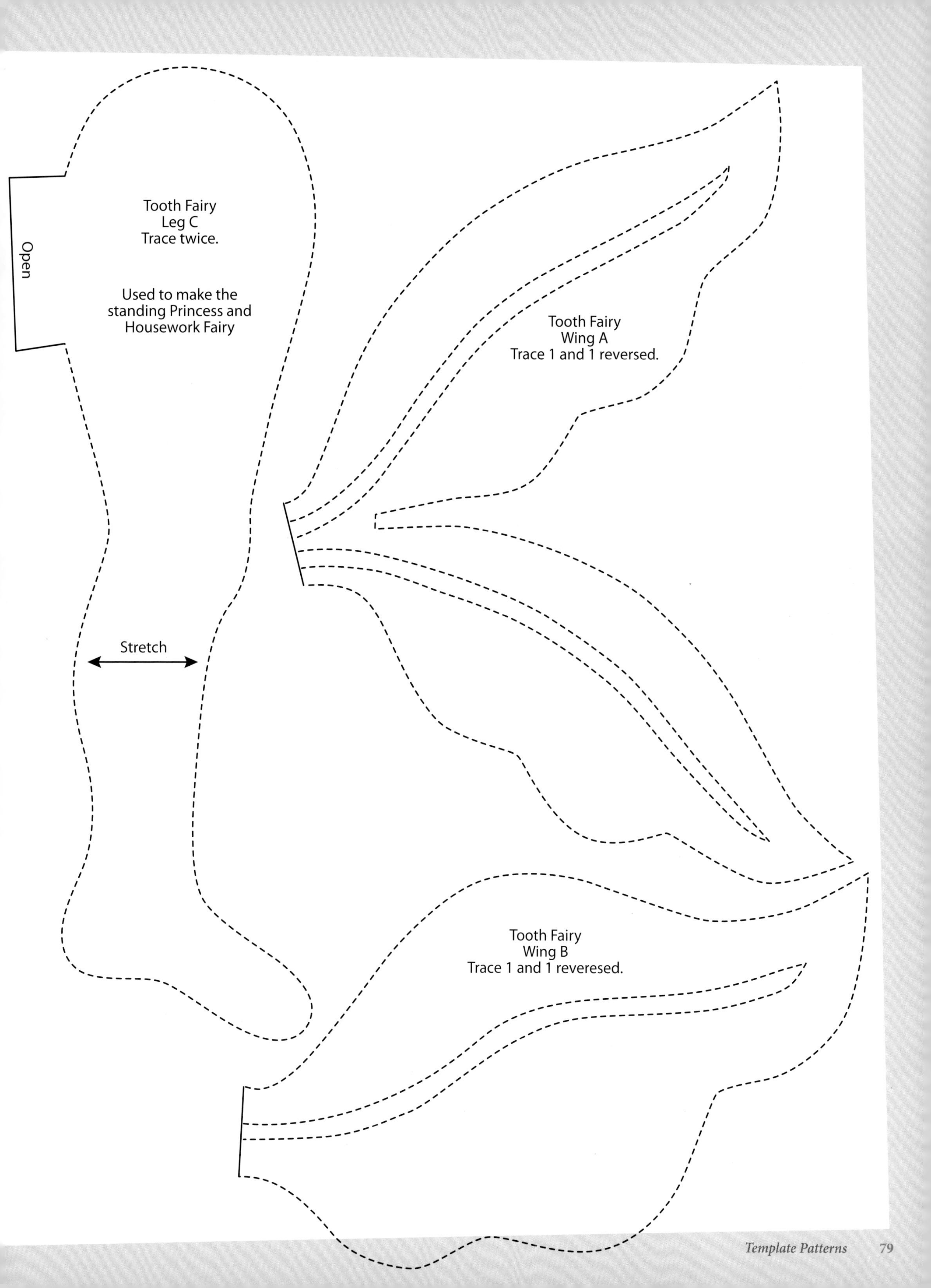
Tooth Fairy
Leg C
Trace twice.
Open
Used to make the
standing Princess and
Housework Fairy
Stretch
Tooth Fairy
Wing A
Trace 1 and 1 reversed.
Tooth Fairy
Wing B
Trace 1 and 1 revereséd.

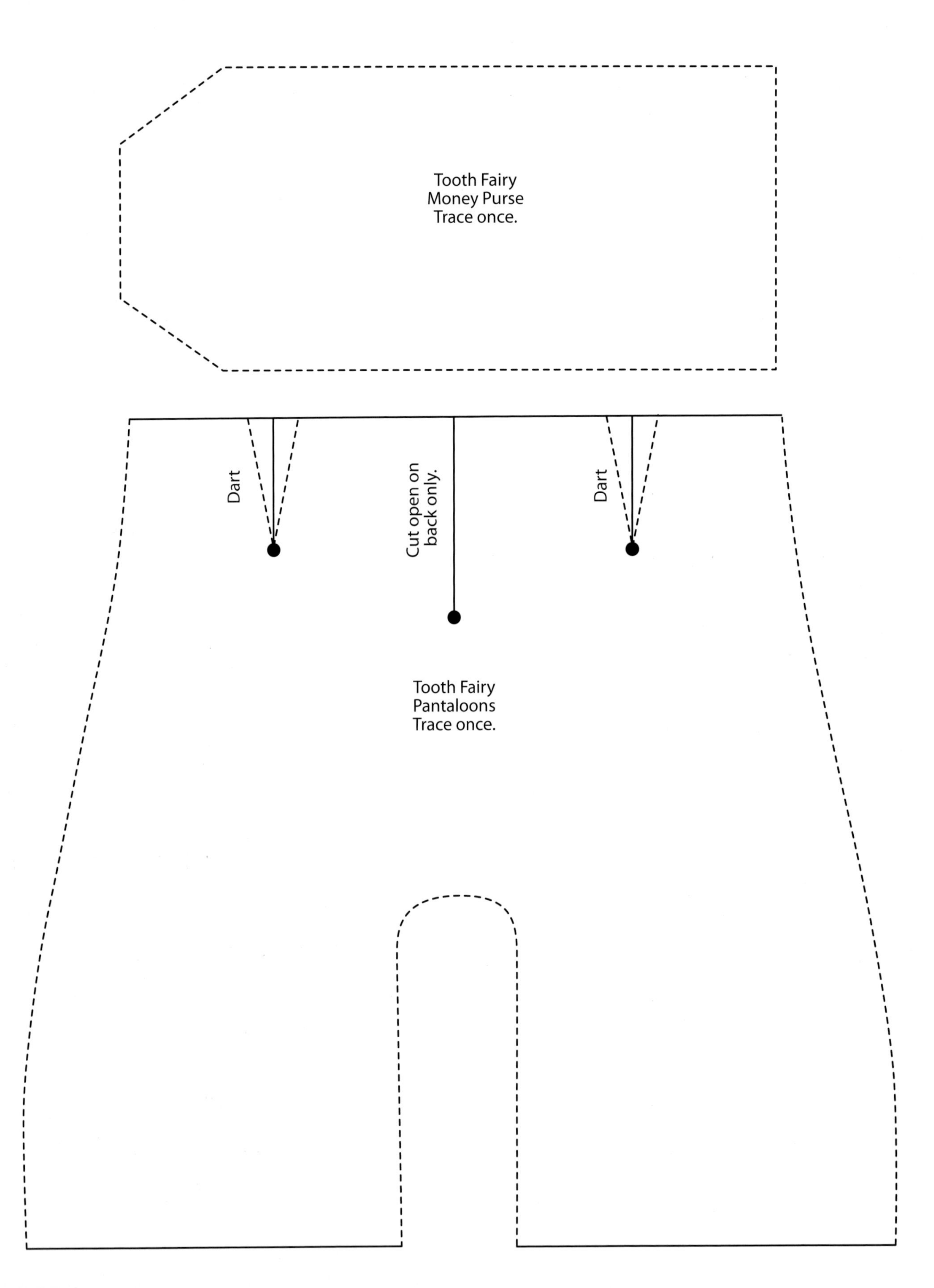
Tooth Fairy
Money Purse
Trace once.
Dart
Cut open on
back only.
Dart
Tooth Fairy
Pantaloons
Trace once.

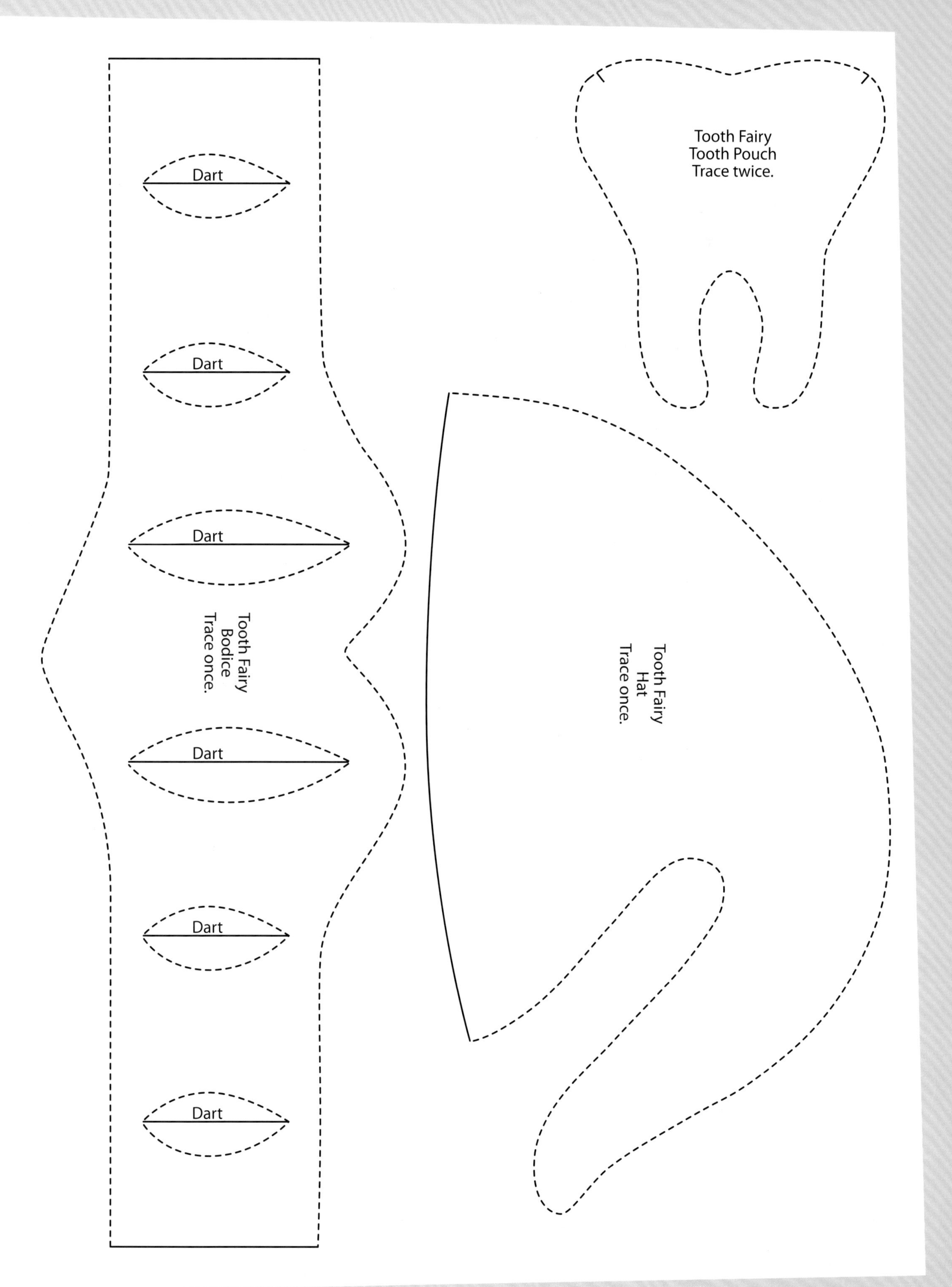
Dart
Dart
Dart
Tooth Fairy
Bodice
Trace once.
Dart
Dart
Dart
Tooth Fairy
Tooth Pouch
Trace twice.
Tooth Fairy
Hat
Trace once.

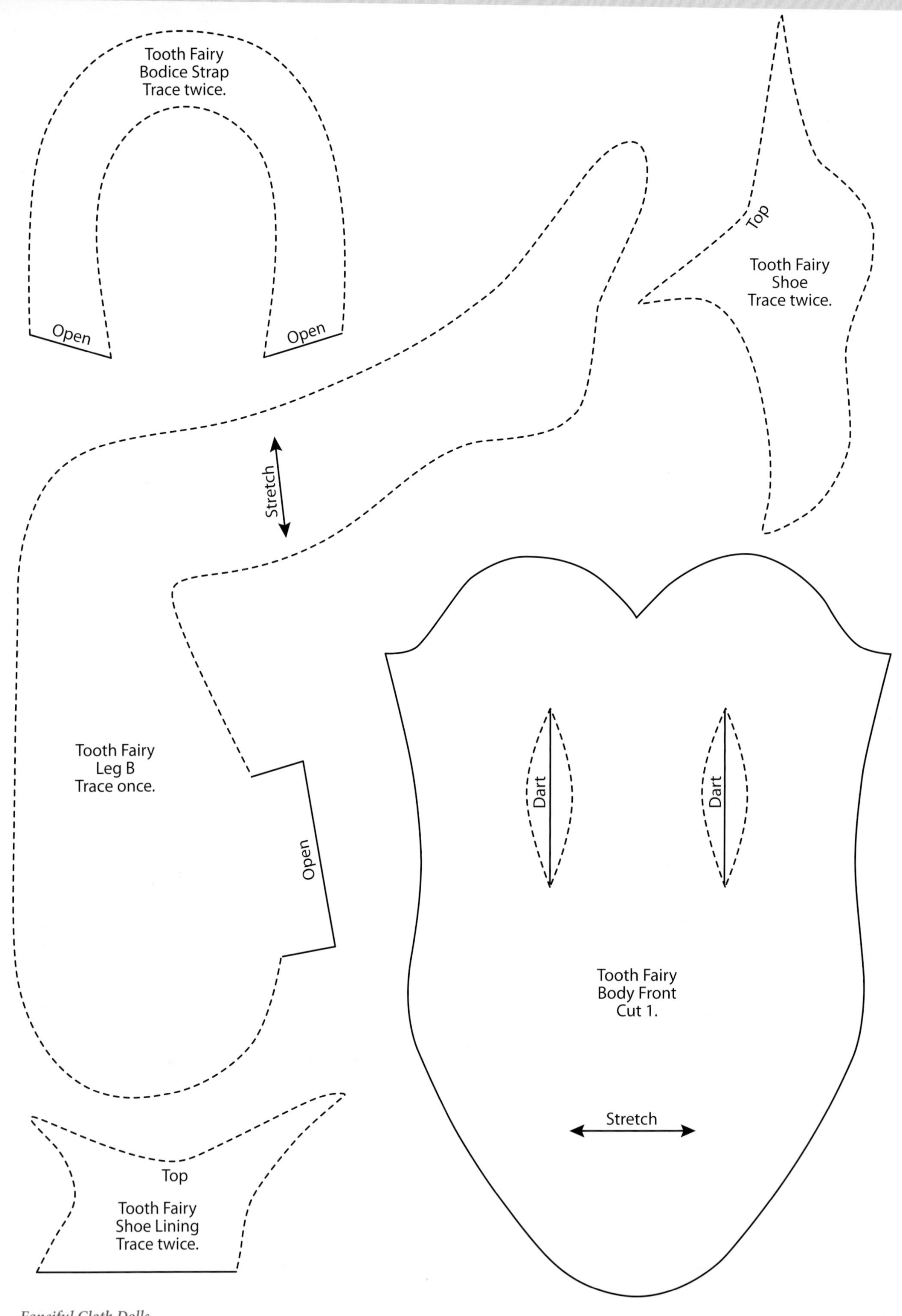
Tooth Fairy
Bodice Strap
Trace twice.
Open
Open
Top
Tooth Fairy
Shoe
Trace twice.
Stretch
Tooth Fairy
Leg B
Trace once.
Open
Dart
Dart
Tooth Fairy
Body Front
Cut 1.
Stretch
Top
Tooth Fairy
Shoe Lining
Trace twice.

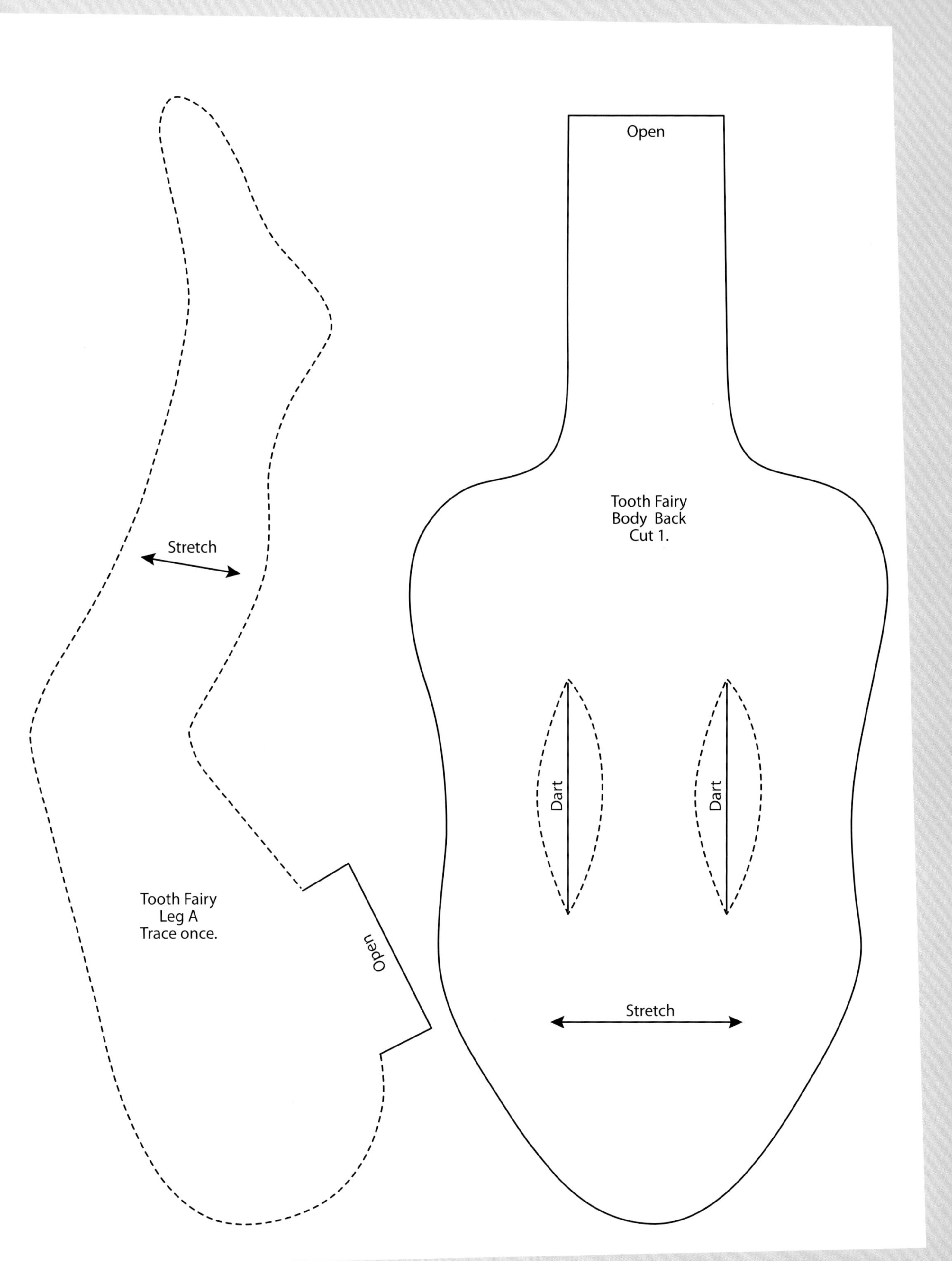
Stretch
Tooth Fairy
Leg A
Trace once.
Open
Open
Tooth Fairy
Body Back
Cut 1.
Dart
Dart
Stretch

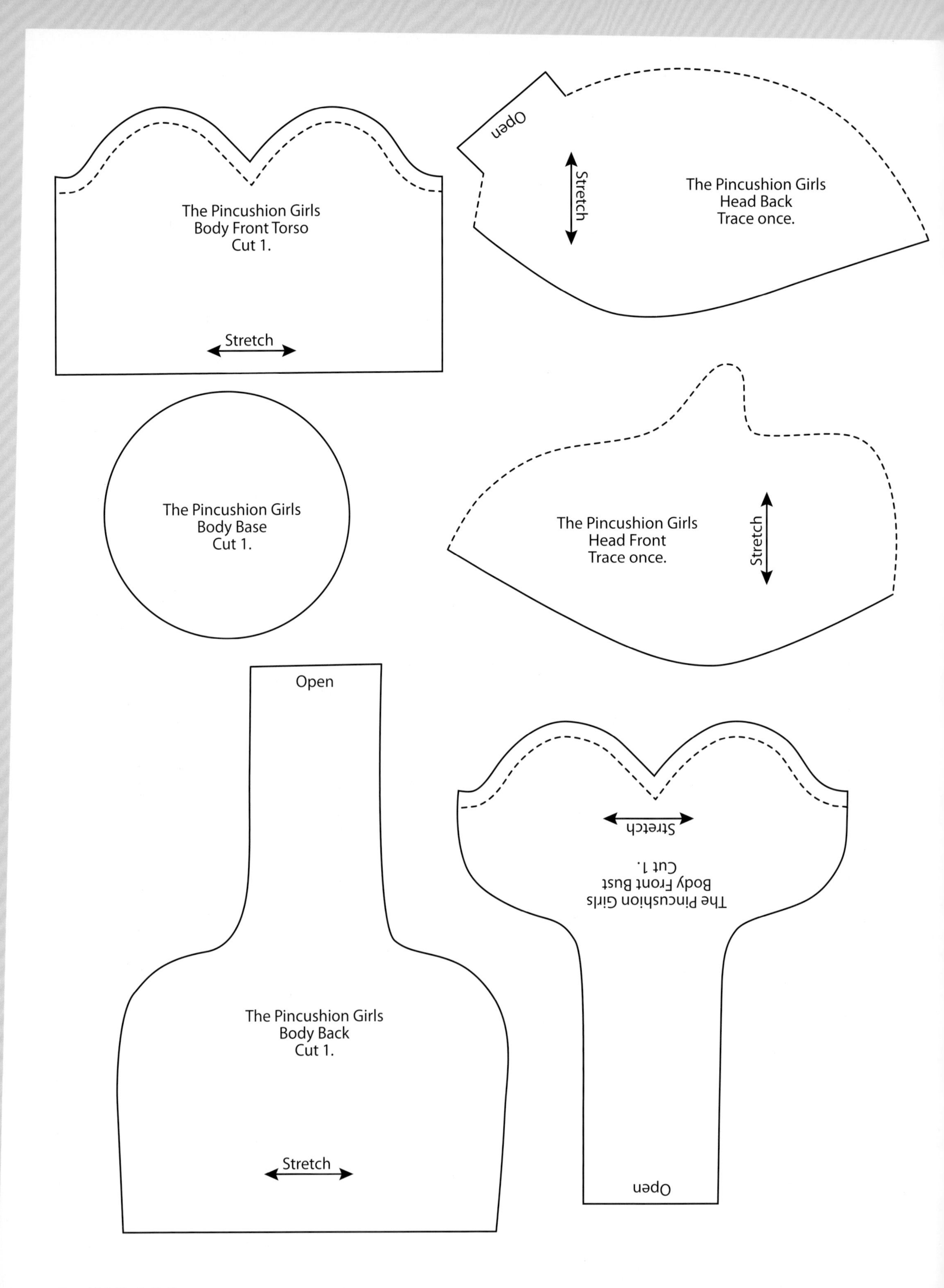
The Pincushion Girls
Body Front Torso
Cut 1.
Stretch
Open
Stretch
The Pincushion Girls
Head Back
Trace once.
The Pincushion Girls
Body Base
Cut 1.
The Pincushion Girls
Head Front
Trace once.
Stretch
Open
The Pincushion Girls
Body Back
Cut 1.
Stretch
Stretch
The Pincushion Girls
Body Front Bust
Cut 1.
Open

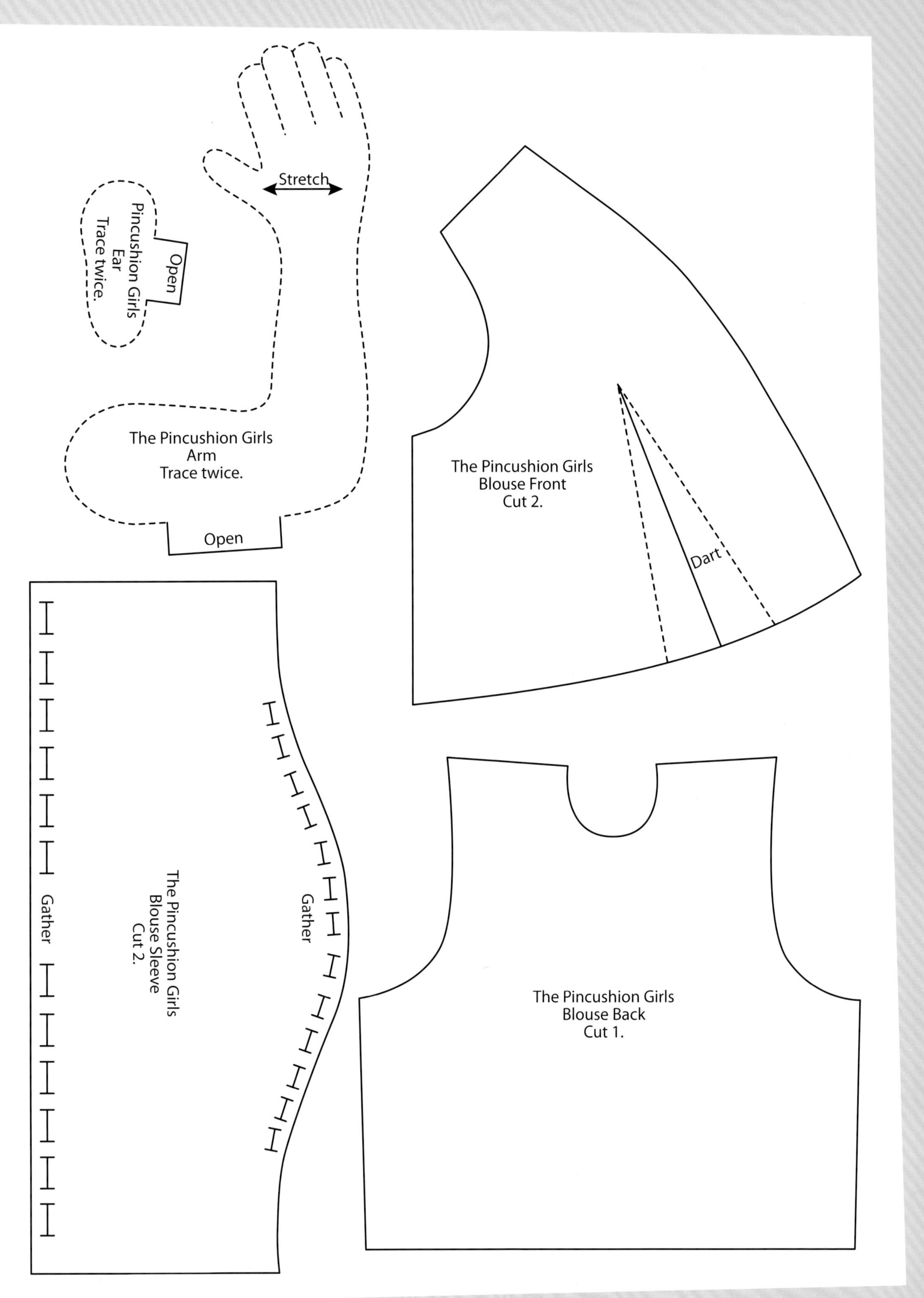
Stretch
Open
Pincushion Girls
Ear
Trace twice.
The Pincushion Girls
Arm
Trace twice.
Open
The Pincushion Girls
Blouse Front
Cut 2.
Dart
Gather
The Pincushion Girls
Blouse Sleeve
Cut 2.
Gather
The Pincushion Girls
Blouse Back
Cut 1.

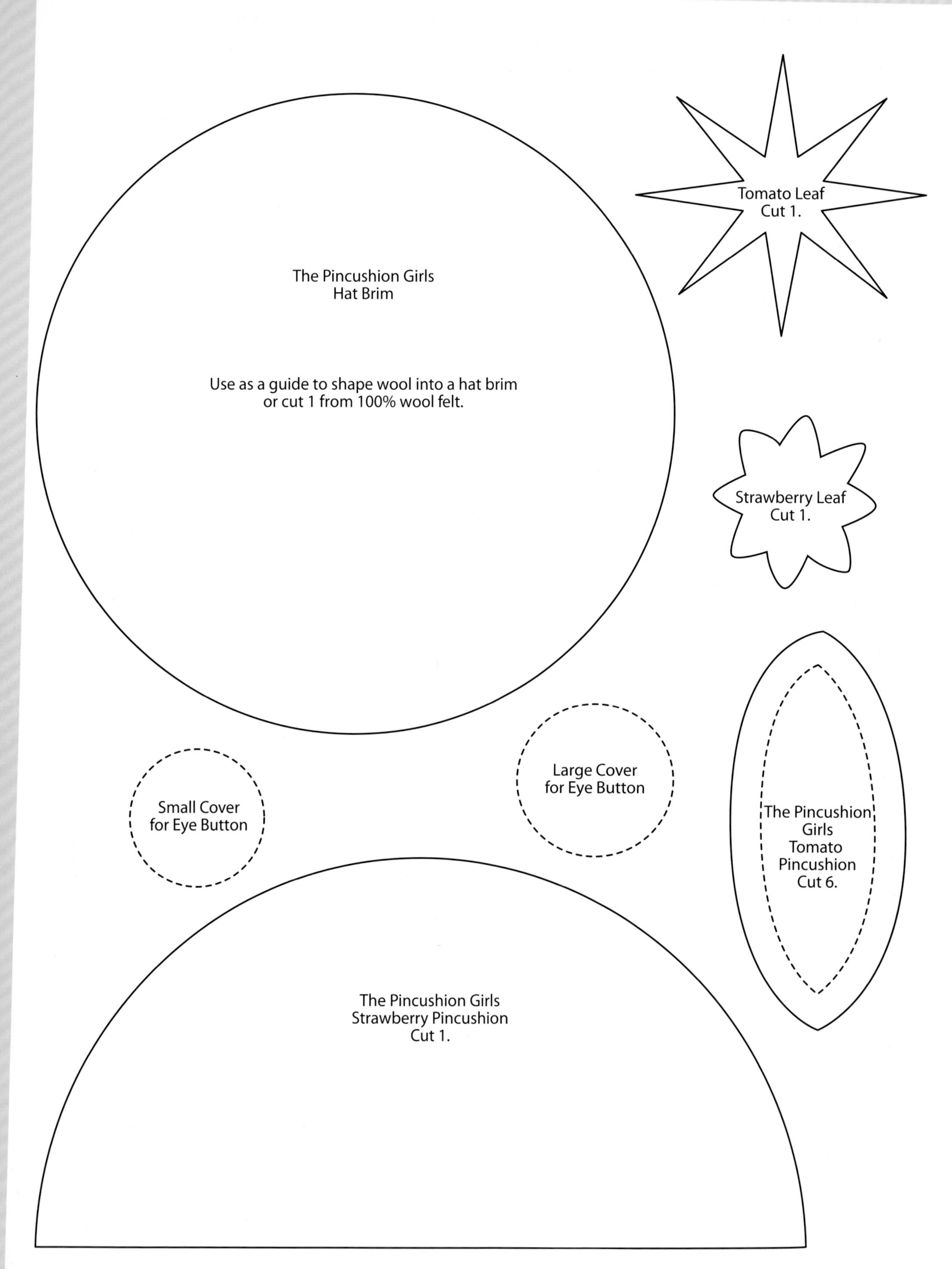
Tomato Leaf
Cut 1.
The Pincushion Girls
Hat Brim
Use as a guide to shape wool into a hat brim
or cut 1 from 100% wool felt.
Strawberry Leaf
Cut 1.
Large Cover
for Eye Button
Small Cover
for Eye Button
The Pincushion
Girls
Tomato
Pincushion
Cut 6.
The Pincushion Girls
Strawberry Pincushion
Cut 1.

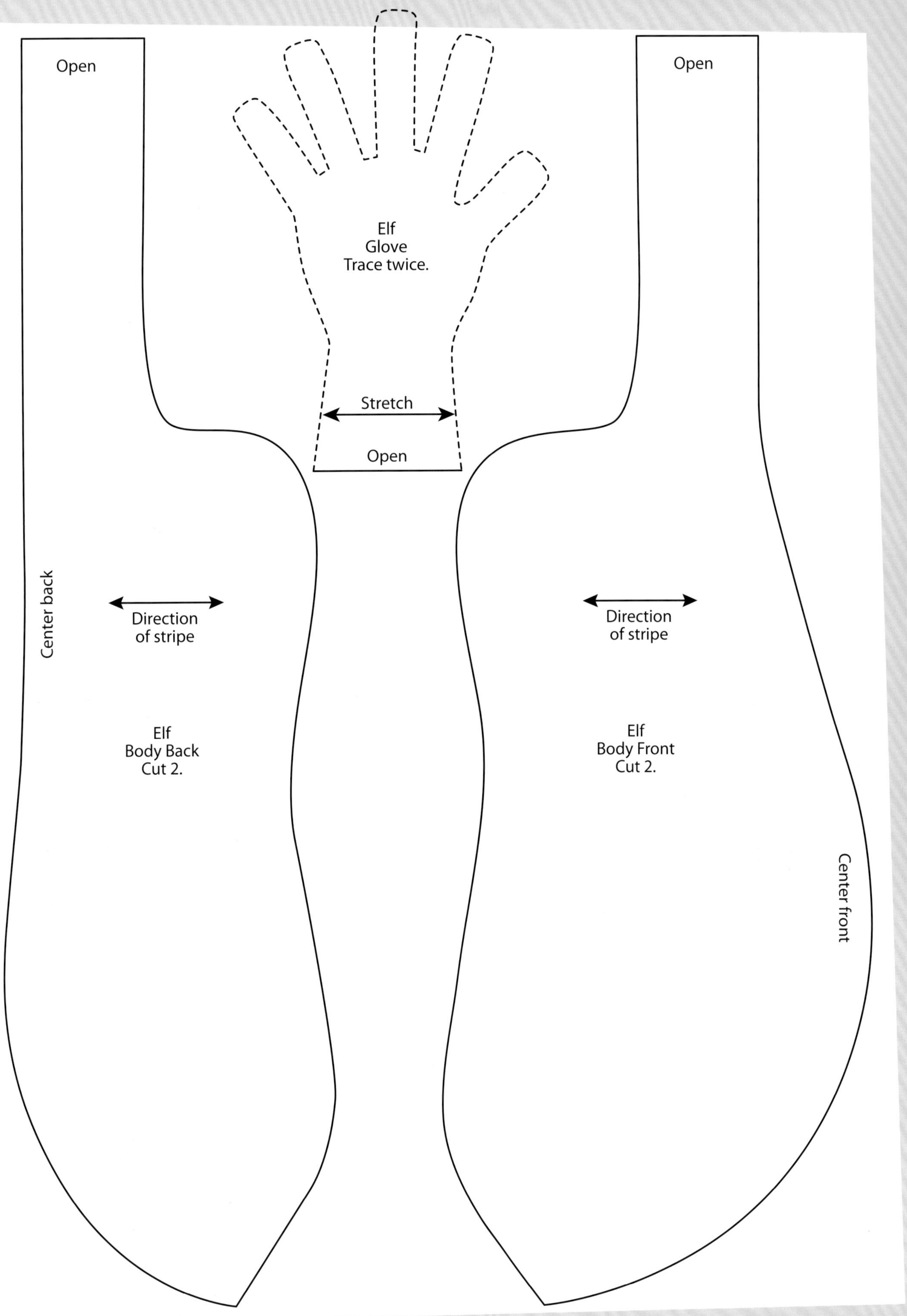
Open
Elf
Glove
Trace twice.
Stretch
Open
Open
Center back
Direction
of stripe
Elf
Body Back
Cut 2.
Direction
of stripe
Elf
Body Front
Cut 2.
Center front

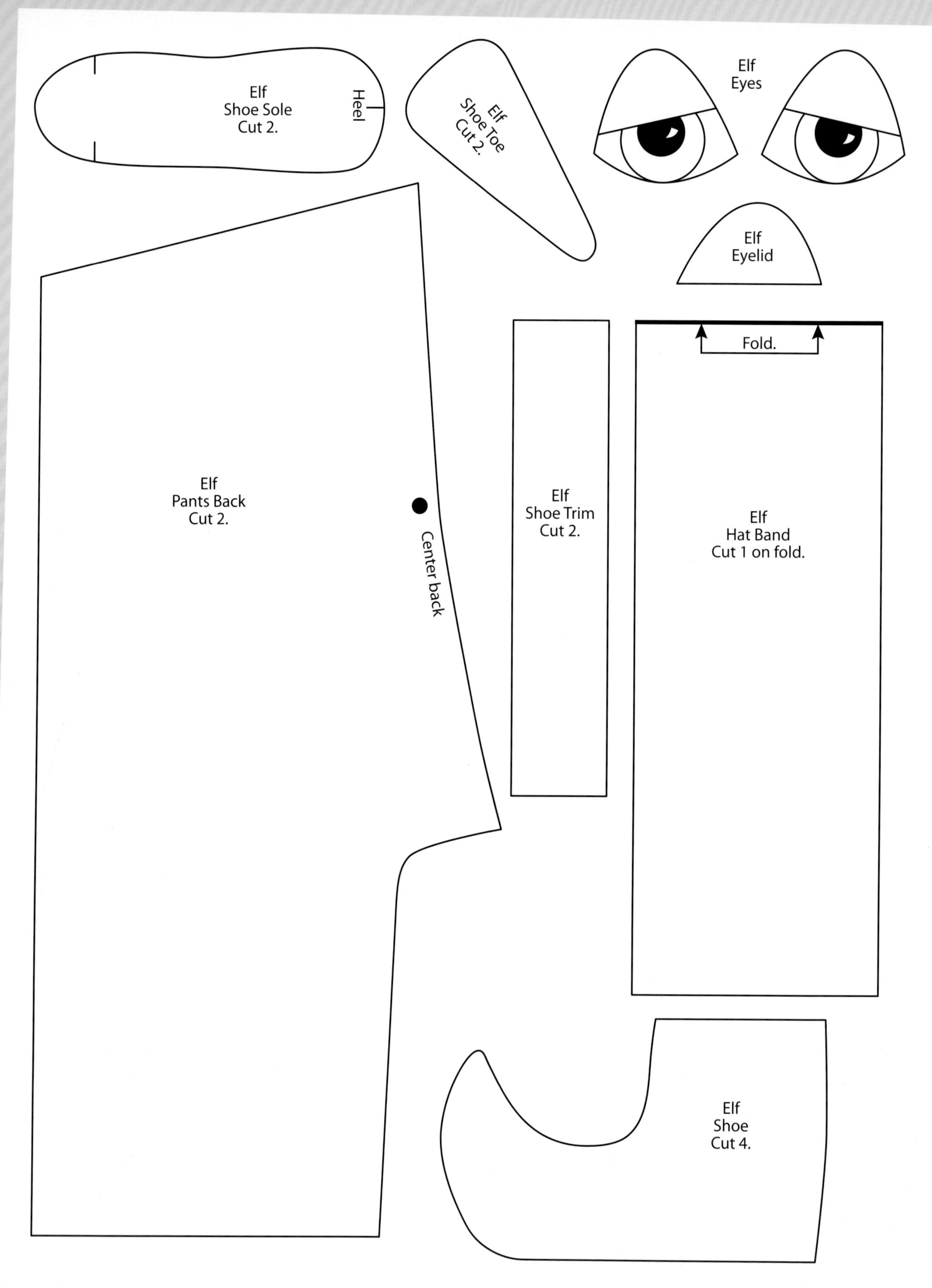
Elf
Shoe Sole
Cut 2.
Heel
Elf
Shoe Toe
Cut 2.
Elf
Eyes
Elf
Eyelid
Fold.
Elf
Pants Back
Cut 2.
Center back
Elf
Shoe Trim
Cut 2.
Elf
Hat Band
Cut 1 on fold.
Elf
Shoe
Cut 4.

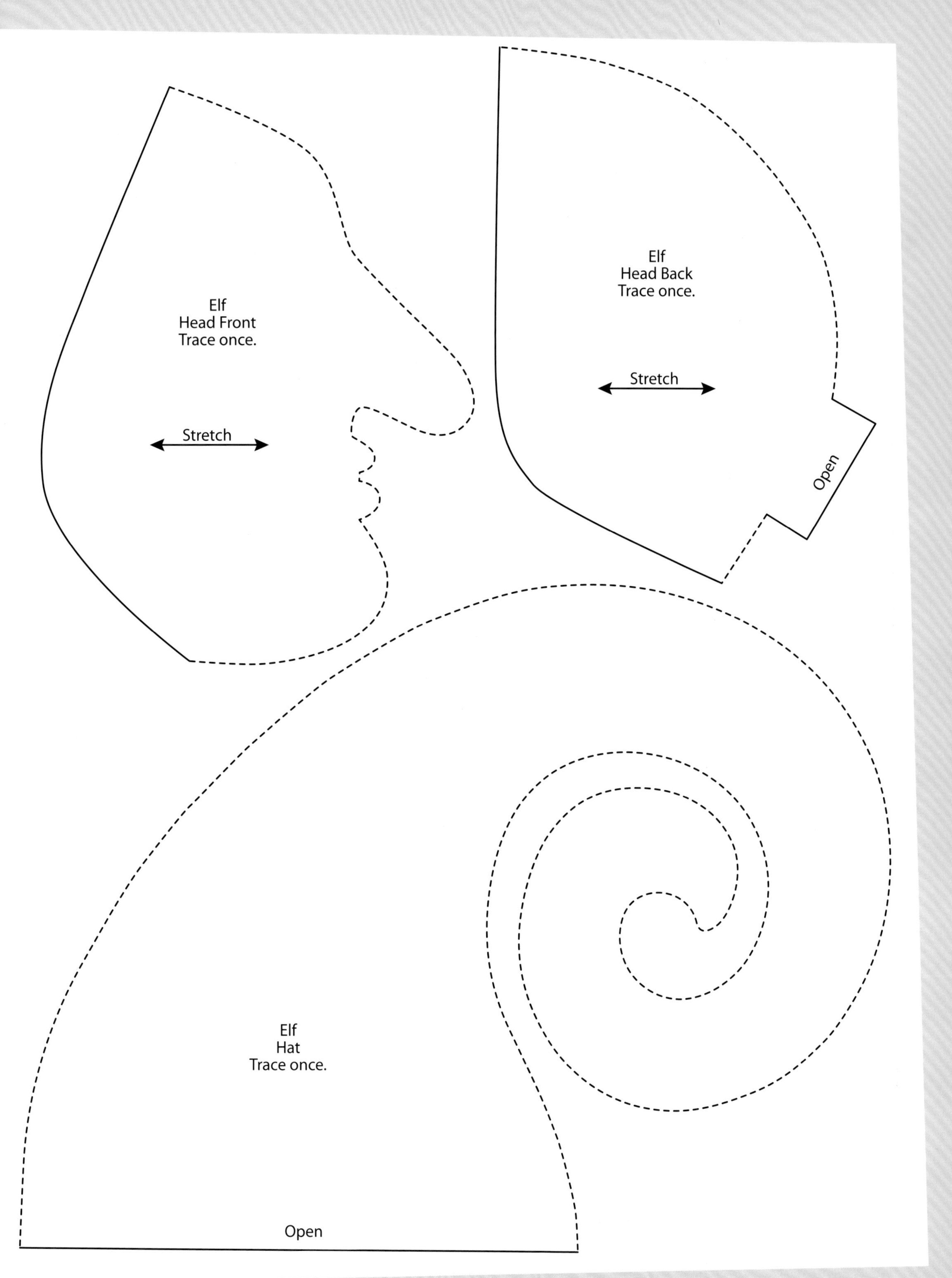
Elf
Head Front
Trace once.
Stretch
Elf
Head Back
Trace once.
Stretch
Open
Elf
Hat
Trace once.
Open

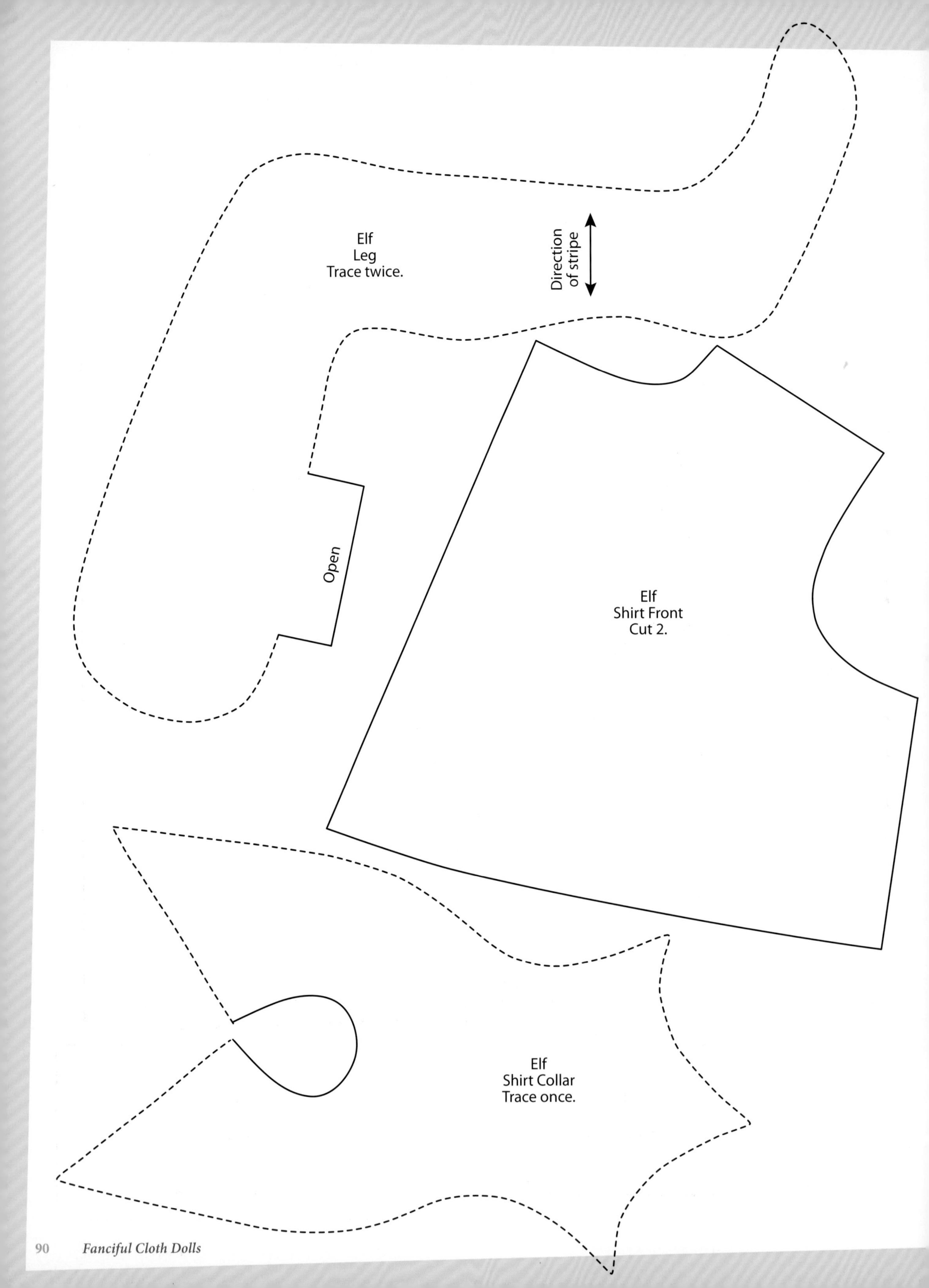
Elf
Leg
Trace twice.
Direction of stripe
Open
Elf
Shirt Front
Cut 2.
Elf
Shirt Collar
Trace once.

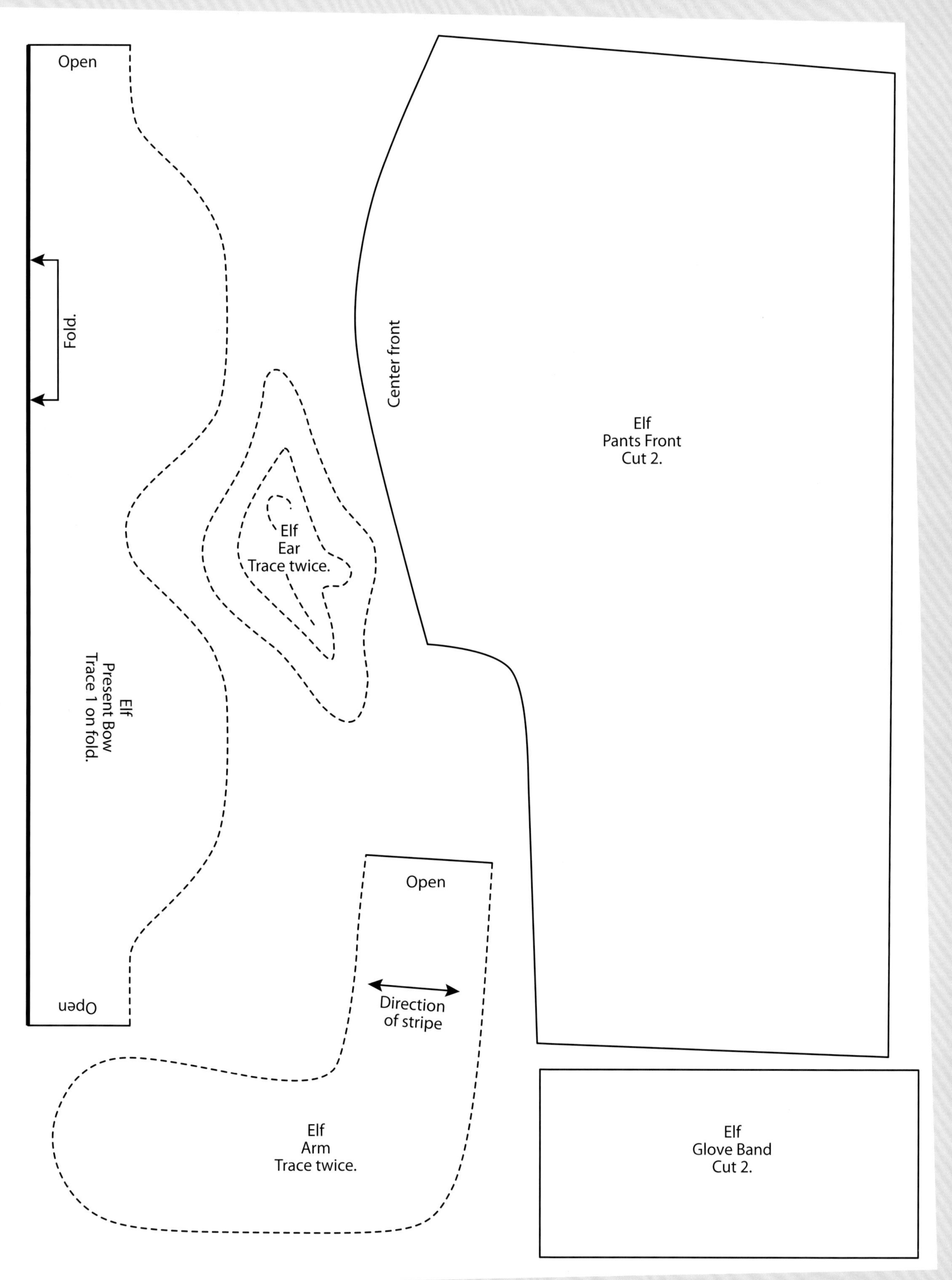
Open
Fold.
Elf
Present Bow
Trace 1 on fold.
Open
Elf
Ear
Trace twice.
Center front
Elf
Pants Front
Cut 2.
Open
Direction
of stripe
Elf
Arm
Trace twice.
Elf
Glove Band
Cut 2.

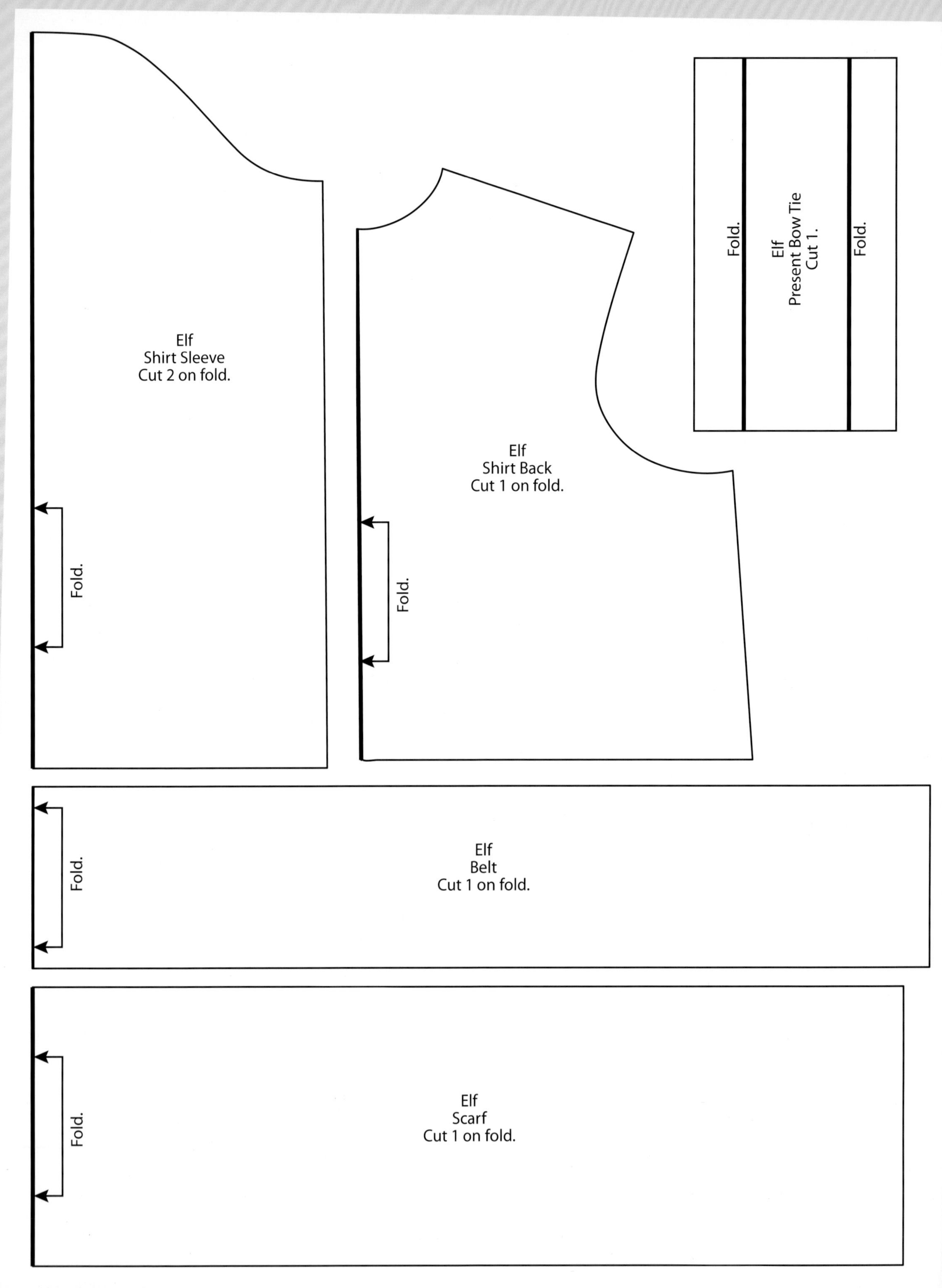
Elf
Shirt Sleeve
Cut 2 on fold.
Fold.
Elf
Shirt Back
Cut 1 on fold.
Fold.
Fold.
Elf
Present Bow Tie
Cut 1.
Fold.
Fold.
Elf
Belt
Cut 1 on fold.
Fold.
Elf
Scarf
Cut 1 on fold.

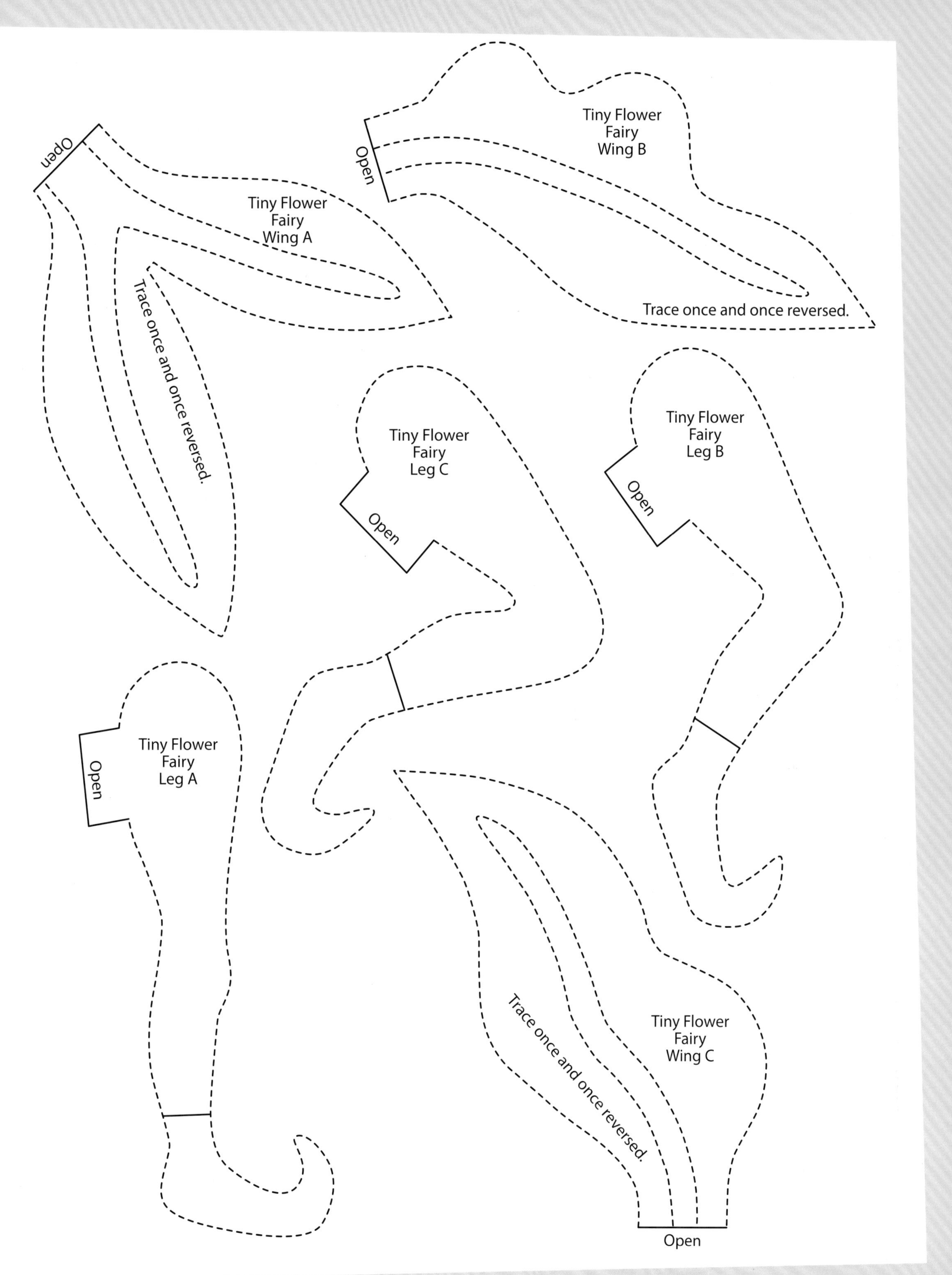
Tiny Flower
Fairy
Wing B
Open
Trace once and once reversed.
Open
Tiny Flower
Fairy
Wing A
Trace once and once reversed.
Tiny Flower
Fairy
Leg C
Open
Tiny Flower
Fairy
Leg B
Open
Tiny Flower
Fairy
Leg A
Open
Trace once and once reversed.
Tiny Flower
Fairy
Wing C
Open

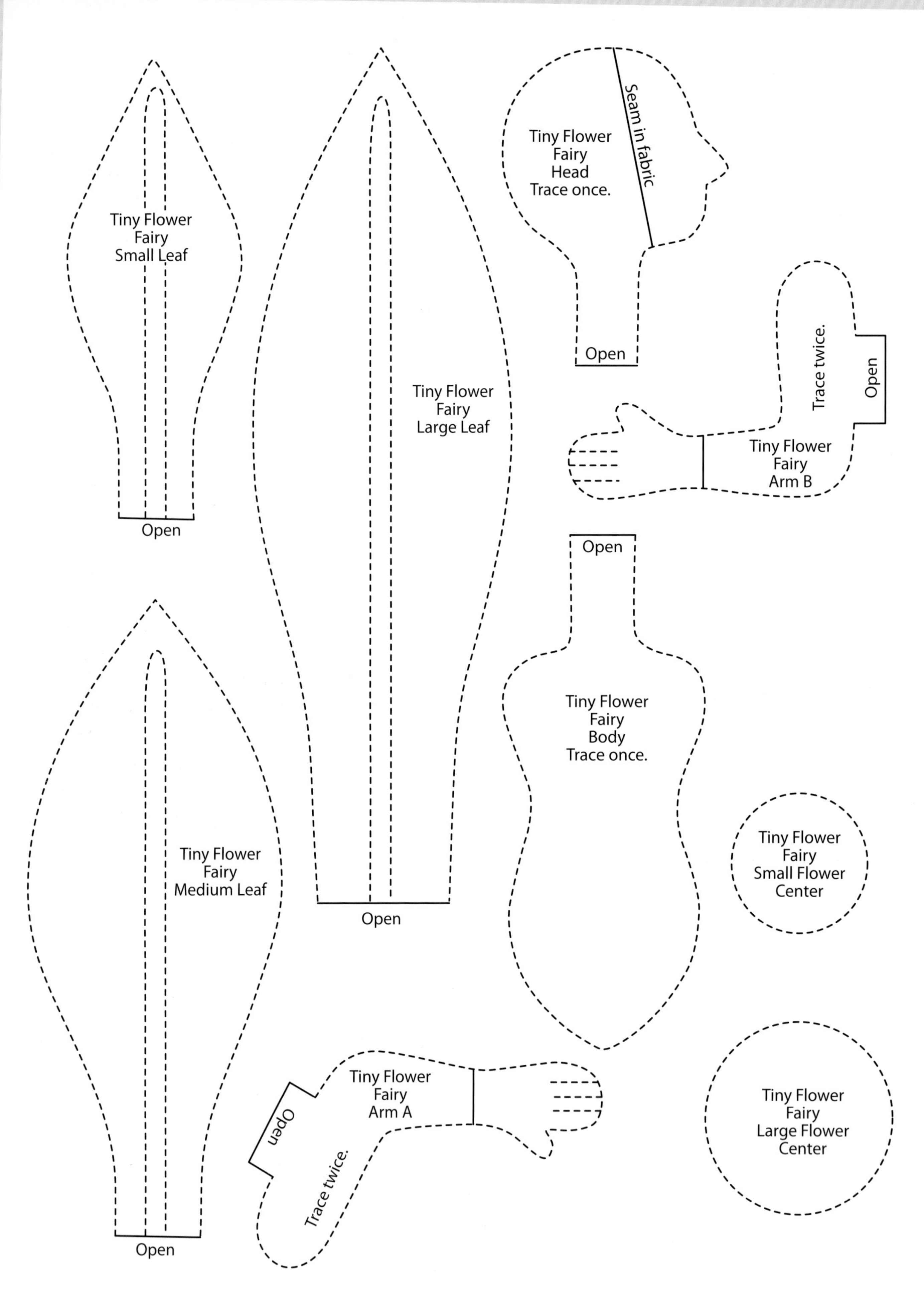
Tiny Flower
Fairy
Small Leaf
Open
Tiny Flower
Fairy
Large Leaf
Open
Tiny Flower
Fairy
Head
Trace once.
Seam in fabric
Open
Trace twice.
Open
Tiny Flower
Fairy
Arm B
Open
Tiny Flower
Fairy
Body
Trace once.
Tiny Flower
Fairy
Medium Leaf
Open
Tiny Flower
Fairy
Small Flower
Center
Tiny Flower
Fairy
Arm A
Open
Trace twice.
Tiny Flower
Fairy
Large Flower
Center

Resources

Turning tubes

Terese Cato
www.teresecato.com

Yarn

Lion Brand Yarn
www.lionbrand.com

Fabric

P&B Textiles
www.pbtex.com

Robert Kaufman Fabrics
www.robertkaufman.com

Timeless Treasures Fabrics
www.ttfabrics.com

Wool batting, roving, curly locks

Dream Felt
www.dreamfelt.com

Lesley Riley's Transfer Artist Paper, Quilter's Vinyl

C&T Publishing
www.ctpub.com

Tooth Fairy tooth pouch (page 34)

Iron-on thread

Kreinik Manufacturing Company
www.kreinik.com

Pincushion Girls blouse detail (page 46)

About the Author

When I was eleven years old, my aunt Marie taught me how to sew, knit, and crochet. Money was scarce when she was young, so her mother made all of her clothes. When Marie got a little older, her mother taught her to sew for herself. There were never any store-bought patterns. Her mother taught her to make her own patterns with a marker and newspapers.

As I think back on it now, I'm sure that if I'd been a bit older I would have told Aunt Marie that it was just too hard! As young as I was, I listened, followed her directions, and did what I was told. Marie had no formal training, only the skills learned from her mother. She taught me how clothes were constructed, and I learned to make patterns with my own marker and stack of newspapers. That was 40 years ago. I know Aunt Marie would be proud to see that I took the skills she taught me and continued to learn and grow.

My mother was an artist. I wanted to be just like her. As a little girl I was in awe of the way she could pick up a pencil and sketch a portrait that looked so real. She was truly gifted, and I worked hard to copy her. I may not have inherited all of her gifts, but I think I got a few of her traits, including hard work and determination. My mother gave me the confidence to become a self-taught artist. I have worked hard to develop the skills to paint, weave, become a woodcarver, and do woodworking. Although my mother has been gone for 28 years, she still inspires me to create, and I feel truly blessed to be able to share what I have learned with others.

Also by Terese Cato:

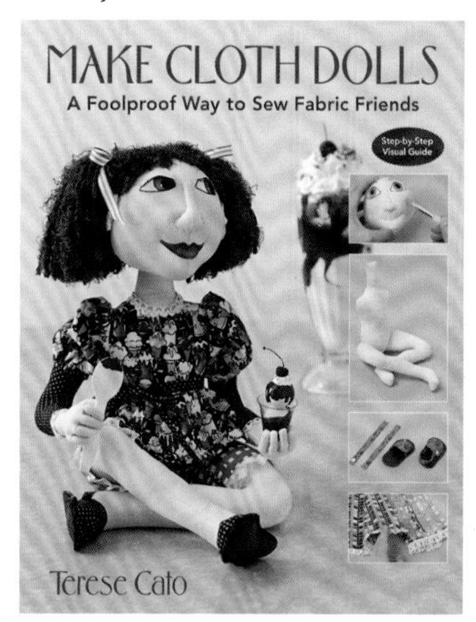

For a list of other fine books from C&T Publishing, visit our website to view our catalog online.

C&T PUBLISHING, INC.
P.O. Box 1456
Lafayette, CA 94549
800-284-1114
Email: ctinfo@ctpub.com
Website: www.ctpub.com

C&T Publishing's professional photography services are now available to the public. Visit us at www.ctmediaservices.com.

Tips and Techniques can be found at www.ctpub.com > Consumer Resources > Quiltmaking Basics: Tips & Techniques for Quiltmaking & More

For quilting supplies:

Note: Fabrics shown may not be currently available, as fabric manufacturers keep most fabrics in print for only a short time.